Internet Concepts

Dr.E. Ramaraj

Dr.K. Kavitha

Published by

Internet Concepts

ISBN 978-93-85477-58-4

Authors

Dr.E. Ramaraj

Dr.K. Kavitha

Bonfring

309, 2nd Floor, 5th Street Extension, Gandhipuram,

Coimbatore-641 012.

Tamilnadu, India.

E-mail: info@bonfring.org

Website: www.bonfring.org

Phone: 0422 4213231

Preface

HTML language is widely used for simple online applications. This book presents basic Networking, HTML and JavaScript in a way that uniquely meets the requirements of students in the sciences and engineering. It explains how to create simple web page and client-side applications for scientific and engineering calculations. It includes many complete HTML/JavaScript examples with science/engineering applications to guide the reader progressively and comprehensively through the subject. Networking Concepts makes also highly suitable for an introductory programming course for non-computer-science majors. Introduction to HTML and JavaScript addresses directly the needs of students by explaining just those components of HTML and JavaScript needed to write their own online applications.

Features and Topics

- Includes detailed code examples and output.
- Extremely accessible and ideal for self-study.
- Offers knowledge of HTML and JavaScript, which are essential for Web development.
- Written specifically to meet the needs of science and engineering students and working professionals.

Unit	Contents	Page No

Unit-I

What is Internet

1.1.   Introduction

Definition of Internet

An internet is defined as a network of networks around the world. It is the largest computer network available and it is used to transfer information through cyberspace. The figure given below shows the structure of a network.

Advantages of internet:

1) Fast communication.
2) Information sharing.
3) Resource sharing.

History of Internet

In 1960, the advanced research project agency (APRA) of US defence department funded a project called APRANET. The aim of the project was to connect universities, computer scientists and engineers through computer and telephone lines.

These project team devices standards to communicate among computers through telephone lines. This was very useful to sent e-mails during war time. This communication is limited only within military and research people.

From late 1980, all the people were allowed to use computer for their communication. In 1989, the world web wide web was invented for connecting the computers around the world. From 1990 the usage of internet facilities spread all over the world.

Networking Models

Networking is a process of connecting computers by means of wire or wireless. The main objective is to share information and resources among computers. Initially, the computer networks were designed with the hardware as the main part and software as its support. But now a day's network software is given more importance. The modern computer networks are designed by the concept of layered protocols or functions. Each layer is built over another. The number of layers, the content of layers and the name of each layer differs from important types of networking models which support different types of networks.

They are:

1) OSI networking model.
2) TCP/IP networking model.

1) OSI Networking Model

The full form of OSI is open system interconnection. This networking model was developed according to the standards of International Standards Organization (ISO). This networking model is used to connect computer systems that are ready to communicate with each other.

Feature of OSI Model

1) Big picture of network is understandable through this OSI model.
2) We see how hardware and software work together.
3) We can understand new technologies as they are developed.
4) Troubleshooting is easier by separate networks.
5) Can be used to compare basic functional relationships on different networks.

OSI model has seven well defined layers to do communication among computers. The figure given below shows the structure of OSI

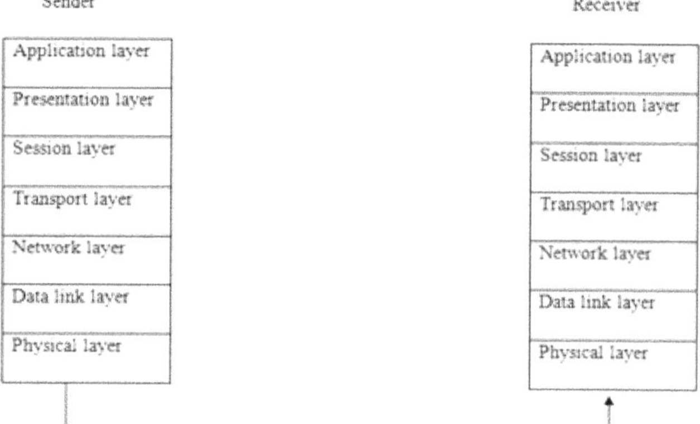

The different layers are

a) Physical Layer

It activates, maintain and deactivate the physical connection. Voltages and data rates needed for transmission is defined in the physical layer. It converts the digital bits into electrical signal.

b) Data Link Layer

Data link layer synchronizes the information which is to be transmitted over the data. Error controlling is easily done. The encoded data are then passed to physical. Error detection bits are used by the data link on layer. It also corrects the errors. Outgoing messages are assembled into frames. Then the system waits for the acknowledgements to be received after the transmission. It is reliable to send message.

c) Network Layer

It routes the signal through different channels to the other end. It acts as a network controller. It decides by which route data should take. It divides the outgoing messages into packets and to assemble incoming packets into messages for higher levels.

d) Transport Layer

It decides if data transmission should be on parallel path or single path. Functions such as multiplexing, segmenting or splitting on the data done by layer four that is transport layer. Transport layer breaks the message (data) into small units so that they are handled more efficiently by the network layer.

e) Session Layer

Session layer manages and synchronize the conversation between two different applications. Transfer of data from one destination to another session layer streams of data are marked and are resynchronized properly, so that the ends of the messages are not cut prematurely and data loss is avoided.

f) Presentation Layer

Presentation layer takes care that the data is sent in such a way that the receiver will understand the information (data) and will be able to use the data. Languages (syntax) can be different of the two communicating systems.

Under this condition presentation layer plays a role translator.

g) Application Layer

It is the top layer. Manipulation of data (information) in various ways is done in this layer. Transferring of files disturbing the results to the user is also done in this layer.

Mail services, directory services, network resource etc are services provided by application layer.

Advantages

1) OSI model distinguish between the services, interfaces and protocols.
2) Protocols of OSI model are very well hidden.
3) They can be replaced by new protocols as technology changes.
4) Supports connection oriented as well as connectionless service.

Disadvantages

1) Model was devised before the invention of protocols.
2) Fitting of protocols is tedious task.

2) TCP/IP Networking Model

The full form of TCP/IP is transmission control protocol/internet protocol. This networking model is used to do communication between networks (internet). This model has four well defined layers as shown below. Each and every layer has a well defined function.

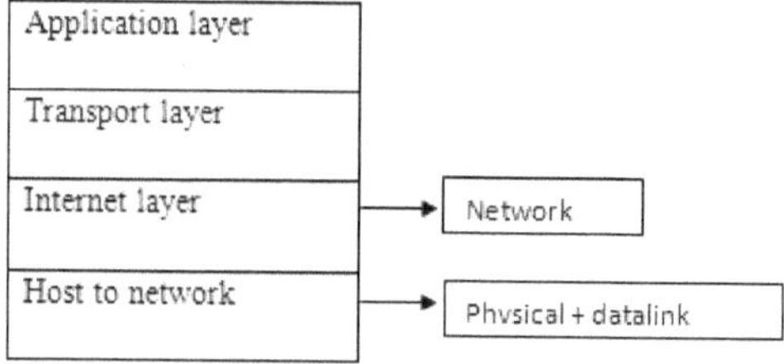

The different layers are

1) Application Layer

This layer contains number of services that are commonly needed by the users. They are

1) File transfer protocol (FTP) to transfer data efficiently from one machine to another.
2) TELNET to log into a remote machine.
3) Electronic mailing facility.
4) Domain name services (DNS) for mapping host names on to their network addresses.
5) NNTP protocol for getting news and articles around the world.
6) HTTP protocol for fetching pages on the WWW.

2) Transport Layer

This layer is used to provide a reliable, cost effective data transport between source and destination machine. For this two protocols are defined in this layer.

They are

1)   Transmission Control Protocol (TCP)
2)   User datagram protocol (UDP)

a) Transmission Control Protocol

This protocol divides the sender information in to discreate message packets. Then it delivers it to the receiver in the internet using a physical connection between them. At the receiving end it reassembles the received message packets into original data. This also controls the data flow between the sender and receiver.

b) User Datagram Protocol

This protocol divides the sender information in to discreate message packets. Then it delivers it to the receiver in the internet without any physical connection between them. So there is no gurantee that the receiver receives all the messages sent by the sender.

3) Internet Layer

This layer is responsible for controlling the operation of the network.

The main functions are:

1)   This defines an official pocket format for the data to send.
2)   To deliver the IP packets from source to destination.
3)   To find the shortest route from sender to receiver.
4)   To control the congestion (dead lock) of packets in the internet.

4) Host to Network Layer

This layer is the lowest layer. The main functions are:

1)   It is responsible for establishing a physical connection (activating, maintaining and deactivating the physical circuit) between the sender and receiver.
2)   It is responsible for sending and receiving I/P packets.

Packet Switching

Packet is defined as a manageable group of data. Packet switching is a process of breaking down the message into small packets and sent across the communication network as independent entities. The figure given below shows the structure of a packet switching network.

Working Principle

The steps given below show how communication takes place between different terminals in the network.

1) The message to sent is broken into packets of equal size. Then in each packet the information such as packet number, address of the receiver etc., are written.
2) The sender places the packets in the communication channel without making a physical connection with the receiver.
3) The routers route the packets to destination in the shortest possible route.
4) In the receiving end the packets won't arrive in the order send by the sender.

Internet Service Provider (ISP)

Internet service provider is a company which offers internet service to their customers. The service may be through dial-up or by any other type. It also provides e-mail accounts to their users. Using this facility the users can sent and receive electronic messages through ISP servers.

Accessing the Internet

In recent years the usage of internet becomes very popular among various sections of the people. The following are the important levels of internet access used by the people.

1) Dial up connection.
2) SLIP/PPP protocols.

1) Dial up Connection

Dial up connection is a link between two computers in the internet using switched telephone network. The user computer is connected to the telephone network with the help of MODEM.

To access the internet MODEM dial to establish a link between the internet service provider (ISP) server. After establishing the link, the user's computer and the hosts machine on the internet can communicate with the help of internet service providers computer IP address.

2) SLIP/PPP Protocols

SLIP/PPP stands for serial line internet protocol/point to point protocol. These two protocols are similar in nature and are used to communicate directly between two computers in the internet using dial-up telephone lines.

For SLIP/PPP internet connection, the following are needed by the user computer.

1) A communication link between the user computer and internet through internet service provider.
2) A networking software to communicate TCP/IP packets information with other computer on the internet.
3) An address namely IP address for identifying the user computer on the internet.

The user computer is connected to the telephone network with the help of MODEM. To access the internet the users MODEM dial to establish a link between the ISP server.

After establishing the link, the user's computer and the host machine on the internet can communicate directly with their own IP address.

ISDN Service

ISDN stands for integrated Services Digital Network or Isolated Subscriber Digital Network. This is designed to provide digital communication. Using this, the user can connect more than one device over a single line. That is designed to provide digital communication using the existing telephone network.

This consists of two 64K speed primary channels of communication. Using this, the used can connect more than one device over a single line. That is we can connect a PC, a phone and a fax (data, voice, video and fax).

The user can perform two tasks simultaneously, such as placing a call and sending a fax or transmitting a data file and receiving a call. By combining the two 64K channels into single 128 K channel, the speed can be increased.

In this, there is no need for digital to analog and analog to digital conversion during communication.

Benefits of ISDN

1) High Speed

This helps to send and receive data four times faster than the ordinary phone lines and modems.

2) Higher Capacity

Since ISDN has two channels for communication, this can be combined to send and receive large files such as pictures, graphs, audio, and video.

3) High Sound and Data Quality

Since the mode of transmission is digital, the voice and sound are very clear without external noices. Error rate will be very low.

4) Cost–Effective

Since the speed is high it is cost effective.

Direct ISP Service through Leased Line

A Leased line is a dedicated telephone line connecting two locations. It is also called as private circuit. Leased lines provide permanent internet service. Leased lines provide a pool of permanent IP addresses for their customers. Normally 16 to 32 IP addresses will be provided. The speed of connection ranges from 64 Kbps to 2mbps. Using leased lines the users can enjoy services like FTP, WWW, DNS and proxy.

Advantages

1) It provides permanent, reliable, high speed internet connectivity compared to dial – up network.
2) ii) The quality of connection is superior to dial – up network.

Disadvantages

1) Very high price.
2) High, threats from viruses, hackers etc because of the permanent connectivity.

Modem

The full form of modem is modulation and demodulation. This is an electronic device which is used to interface computers and telephone network. This converts the digital signal from computer to analog and analog signal from network to digital.

The digital data from sender side computer is converted to analog data by the modem and is transmitted over telephone line. This is called modulation. On the receiver side the analog data is converted into digital data by the modem and is given to the receiver computer. This is called demodulation.

Cable Modem

Cable modem is a device used to connect computer to a local cable TV line. It does the modulation and demodulation between analog and digital signal as ordinary modem. But it is more complex than ordinary modem. All cable modem has its IP address. Using this address the modem can transfer data between hosts in the internet. These modems support 1.5 mbs of data transfer.

Internet Tools

Internet tools are tools (software) used for information retrieval, interaction and communication.

The most commonly used tools are:

1) search engines
2) web browser

Search Engines

Search engines is a software tool used to search for a particular information on the internet. Each web site has its own search engines.

The following are the most commonly used search engines.

1) Google
2) Alta vista
3) Northern light

Features of Search Engines

1) It maintains a huge database
2) The database contains an index which covers all the words, titles, URL's etc.
3) Each index is linked with the corresponding address which contains the information.
4) The search engines up dates the indices at regular intervals.

Web Browser

Web browser is a software program in the client machine. This is used to search information on the web site. The browser used HTTP protocol to request information from the web server.

The most commonly used web browsers are:

1) Internet explorer
2) Netscape navigator
3) Mozilla
4) Opera

Features

1) Web browsers allow the users to access information given in many web pages   using links.

2) Web browsers format html information for display. So the appearance of the web page differs from browsers.

3) Web browsers contain number of buttons such as back button, forward button, close box, history button, home button etc to do operation easy.

1.2.   Internet Protocol

Internet Protocol (IP)

Internet is defined as an inter connection of autonomous computers located at different points. To make communication among these computers, We are in need of communication standards (structure, etc). These standards are called Protocols. Therefore Internet protocol (IP) is defined as a standard used for communicating data packets (data grams) from source to destination using internet.

In general internet protocol (IP) takes care of handling the actual delivery of data.

The figure given below shows the structure of 32 bit IP diagram.

◄─────────────── 32 bits ───────────────►

Version	IHL	Type of service	Total Length	
4	4	8	16	
Identification 16			Flag 3	Fragment offset 13
Time to live 8	Protocol 8		Header checksum 16	
	Source IP address		32	
	Destination IP address		32	
	options		32	
	Data		32	

The different fields of IP datagram are

Version

It contains the version of the protocol used. For example IPV4, IPB6.

IHL

It contains the length of the datagram header in 32 bit length.

Types of Service

This is used to tell the subnet about the service it wants.

For example, for file transfer, error free transmission is more important than fast transmission.

Total Length

This field contains total length of the datagram including header and data. The maximum length is 65,535 bytes.

Identification

The identification number helps the destination in reassembling the datagram.

Flag

This is a three bit field. First bit is reserved. The next bit is called do not fragment the datagram because, the destination is incapable of putting the pieces back together again. If 0, the datagram will be fragmented.

Fragment Offset

This value tells the relative position of the fragment (portion) within the datagram.

Time to Live

This value is used to control the packet life time. This contains a counter. For each hop (jump) from one router to other the counter value will be decremented.

Protocol

This field defines the higher level protocol that uses the services of IP layer.

Header Checksum

This value is used to check the errors generated by bad memory words inside a router.

Destination Address

IP address of the destination.

Source Address

IP address of the source.

Option

This field is used for network testing and debugging.

Data

This field contains the user data to be send to the destination.

IP Addresses

IP addresses are used to identify the computers connected in the internet. All internet communications are taking place with the help of this address only.

IP address is a 32 bit binary number containing 4 values of each 8 bits, separated by a decimal point. The structure of IP address is,

Value1, Value2, Value3, Value4

There are two common ways to give IP address. They are:

1) Dotted Decimal Notation

In this, each value is represented by decimal number 0 to 255 separated by decimal points. These numbers are called octests.

Example: 140.179.220.200

2) Binary Notation

In this each value is represented by 8 bit binary numbers separated by decimal points.

Example: 10001100. 10110011.11011100.11001000

All IP address consists of two parts. They are:

1) A part to identify the network address
2) A part of identify the host address

Types of Internet Addressing

There are two types of internet addressing. They are:

1) Classful addressing.
2) Classless addressing.

1) Classful Addressing

In this type of addressing, the network number field is divided into five classes. Each class contains a different network number. The table given below list the number of networks supported by the address and the number of hosts addressed by each class.

Example

1) 127.255.255.255 –class A address

2) 192.88.99.0-class C address

2) Classless Addressing

In this type of addressing, the whole address space is divided into blocks of different sizes. Each address block is given o organization depending on their need. The organizations can use the block of IP addresses for their communication.

Transmission Control Protocol (TCP)

Transmission control protocol is a set of rules used to send data between computers over the internet. TCP and IP are tied together as TCP/IP and are used to send data between computers. The internet protocol(IP) takes care of handling the actual delivery of data. But TCP takes care of keeping track of the individual units of data(message or data packets). TCP provides reliable, ordered delivery of stream of bytes from one system to another system. It also provides facilities like e-mail, file transfer etc.

TCP transfers data between two systems in terms of segments or data segments or data packets. Segment consists of fixed number of bytes. The figure given below shows the structure of TCP data segment.

<table>
<tr><td colspan="8">Source port address

16</td><td colspan="2">Destination port address

16</td></tr>
<tr><td colspan="8"></td><td colspan="2">Sequence number(32)</td></tr>
<tr><td colspan="8">Acknowledge number(32)</td><td colspan="2"></td></tr>
<tr><td>Data

Offset(4)</td><td>Reserved

(6)</td><td>U
R
G</td><td>A
C
K</td><td>P
S
H</td><td>R
S
T</td><td>S
Y
N</td><td>F
1
N</td><td colspan="2">Window size (32)</td></tr>
<tr><td>Checksum(16)</td><td></td><td></td><td></td><td></td><td></td><td></td><td></td><td colspan="2">Urgent pointer(16)</td></tr>
<tr><td>Options and padding</td><td></td><td></td><td></td><td></td><td></td><td></td><td></td><td colspan="2"></td></tr>
<tr><td>Data</td><td></td><td></td><td></td><td></td><td></td><td></td><td></td><td colspan="2"></td></tr>
</table>

←————————————— **32 bit** —————————————→

The different fields are

Source Port Address

This field contains the address of sending port.

Destination Port Address

This field contains the address of receiving port.

Sequence Number

This field specifies the number of the initial segment send. This value is used for numbering the subsequent data to send. (That is sequence number value +1)

Acknowledgement

This field specifies the acknowledgement about the data segment received.

Data Offset

It contains the length of the TCP segment in 32 bit length.

Reserved

This field is reserved for future use.

Flags

There a six flag fields. They are:

UGR –This indicates that urgent pointer field is significant

ACK- This indicates that acknowledge field is significant

PSH- This indicates that the data must be pushed

RST- This indicates that connection is to be reset

SYN- This indicates to synchronize sequence numbers

Window Size

This specifies the number of bytes the receiver is currently willing to receive.

Checksum

This field is used for error checking of header and data.

Urgent Pointer

This field is valid only when URG flag is set.

Options

This field is used to include optional information in TCP header.

Unit–II

HTML

2.1. Introduction to HTML

What is HTML

HTML is a markup language for describing web documents (web pages).

1) HTML stands for Hyper Text Markup Language.

2) A markup language is a set of markup tags.

3) HTML documents are described by HTML tags.

4) Each HTML tag describes different document content.

HTML stands for hyper text markup language. This language is used for creating and displaying web pages using any web browser like internet explorer, netscap navigator etc. This was developed by Tim Berness Lee of European center for particle physics in the year 1989. The following gives the meaning of HTML.

1) Hypertext: This is ordinary text dressed up with extra features like formatting, images, multimedia and links to other documents.

2) Markup: It is a process of taking ordinary text and adding extra symbols. Each symbol used for markup in HTML is a command that tells the browser about its display.

3) Language: HTML is a computer language like C, java etc. It has its own syntax, and rules for proper communication.

Using HTML we can markup our document by indicating the different parts of our document by functions. According to this the browser displays the document anywhere in the world.

Structure of HTML Document

The general form of the HTML document is

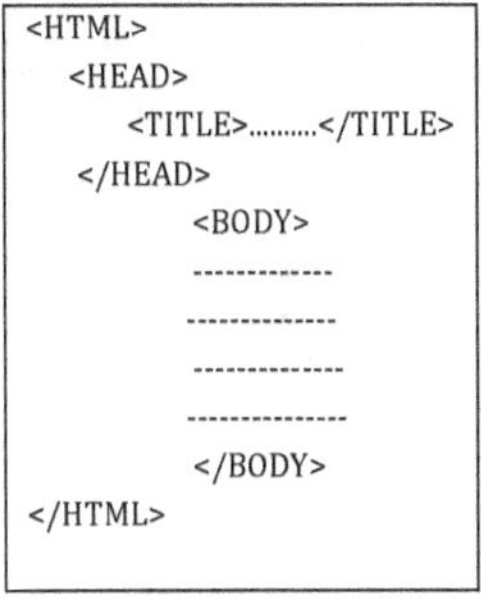

```
<HTML>
   <HEAD>
         <TITLE>..........</TITLE>
   </HEAD>
            <BODY>
            --------------
            --------------
            --------------
            --------------
            </BODY>
</HTML>
```

<HTML>---------</HTML> : All HTML documents must begin with opening tag <HTML> and ends with closing tag </HTML>

Head Section : This section is used to display the title of the HTML document. This section begins with opening tag <HEAD> and ends with closing tag </HEAD>

<TITLE>----------</TITLE> : The title of the HTML document is defined within the tags. This will be displayed in the title bar of the window.

Body Section : This section is used to give any information. This section begins with opening tag <BODY> and ends with closing tag </BODY>. These information's will be displayed in the web page.

Example

```
<HTML>
   <HEAD>
       <TITLE>..........</TITLE>
   </HEAD>
          <BODY>
          COURSE OFFERED
       1)  civil
       2)  mechanical
       3)  information technology
        </BODY>
</HTML>
```

Tools required

To create a document, the following tools are required.

1) Editor : It is a tool to create a html document. The commonly used editors are notepad, word, edit etc. The created document is converted and stored as ASCII text file.
2) Browser : It is a tool used to run the created html document. The commonly used editors are internet explorer, netscape navigator.
3) Special tools : These tools are used to create, run and to host html documents. The commonly used tools are MS Front page, netscape composer etc.

Basic tags of HTML. The important basic tags are:

1) HTML
2) HEAD

3) TITLE

4) BODY

1) *HTML tag*

HTML tag is used to fix the beginning and end of an HTML document. The general form is

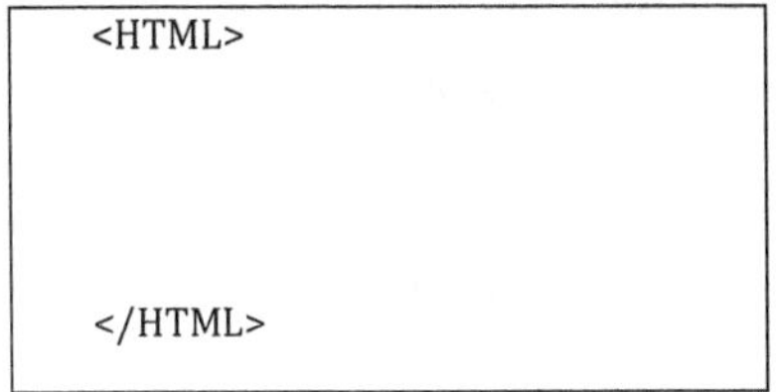

Where

    <HTML> - opening tag

    </HTML> - closing tag

All HTML programs must start with the tag <HTML> and end with the tag </HTML>.

2) *HEAD tag*

HEAD tag is used to describe the content of the HTML document and it is an optional tag. It is like a cover page of a document. The information contained in the HEAD tag is generally referred as meta information.

The general form is:

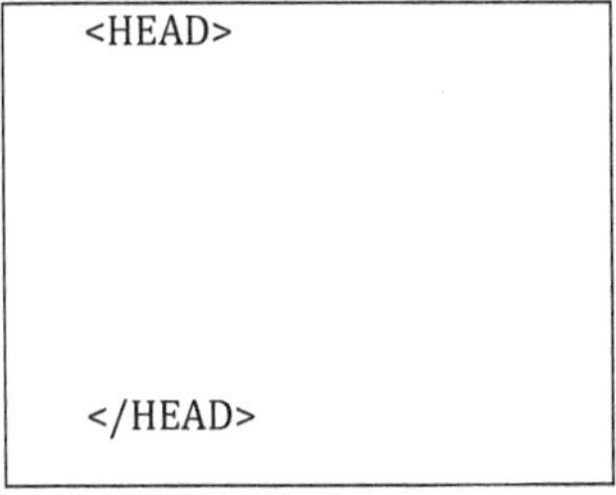

Where

    <HEAD> - opening tag

    </HEAD> - closing tag

3) *TITLE tag*

TITLE tag is used to define the title of the html document. This is included with in the HEAD tag. The information given in this tag is displayed in the title bar of the window.

The general form is

<TITLE>

Title of the document

</TITLE>

Where

<TITLE>- opening tag

</TITLE>-closing tag

In html documents then must be only one title element.

Examples

```
<HTML>
<HEAD>
<TITLE>My first html program
</TITLE>
</HEAD>
</HTML>
```

The information My first html program will be displayed in the title bar.

4) *BODY tag*

BODY tag contains the information to be displayed in the page.

The general form is:

<BODY attribute = "VALUE">

Information to be displayed in the web page

</BODY>

The attributes are:

1) BACKGROUND : This attribute is used to set a background image.

2) BGCOLOR : This attribute is used to set a background color.

3) TEXT : This attribute is used to set the colour of the text to be displayed.

4) VLINK : This attribute is used to set the colour for the visited links.

5) TOP MARGIN : This attribute is used to set the top margin between the browser window and its content.

6) LEFT MARGIN : This attribute is used to set a left margin between the browser window and its content.

Example

(i) <BODY BACKGROUND = "clouds.jpg">

(ii)

    WELCOME

    </BODY>

The information WELCOME will be displayed with a cloud background image.

(iii) <BODY BGCOLOR ="BLACK"TEXT="WHITE">

    WELCOME

    </BODY>

The information WELCOME will be displayed with while text and black background colour.

Creating a HTML Document

Steps to be followed to create a HTML document are:

1) Click start button from windows task bar. This displays a pull down menu.

2) From this, select programs and then select accessories from the next pull down menu. From the next pull down menu click to select notepad. This displays the following window.

3) Within the notepad window type the HTML code as shown below

4) Select File and click the save option. Type the file name with extension HTML. For example abc.html.

5) Open the web browser internet explorer, and is shown below.

6) Select file and open the stored HTML file abc.html. This displays the web page and is shown below. The title of the document XYZ POLYTECHNIC given between the tags <TITLE>....</TITLE> is displayed on the title bar.

7) If any error occurs in the displayed page, it can be corrected by selecting source from view menu in the web browser. It displays the source document in the notepad. Correct the errors and save them. With the help of refresh button we can run the source code directly to get the result.

Formatting of Text

Formatting is a process of presenting the information in the html document in an attractive way.

This is done with the help of the available html formatting tags.

Header Tag

These tags are used to give headings in HTML documents. There are six levels of heading in HTML. Each level has its own font size. They are

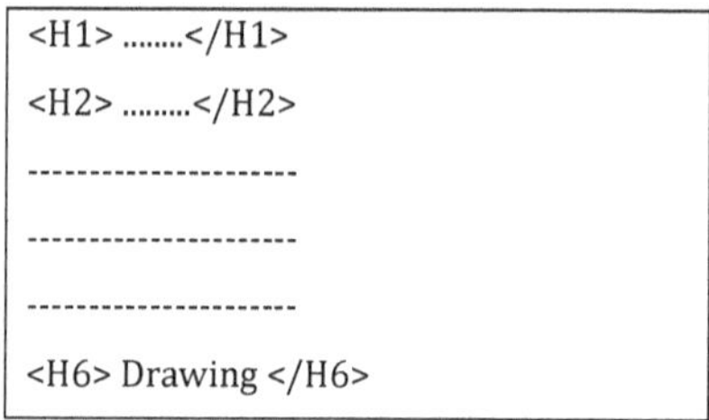

Example

```
<H1> BCS </H1>
<H2> Physics </H2>
<H3>Chemistry </H3>
<H4>Maths 1</H4>
<H5> Maths 2 </H5>
<H6> Drawing </H6>
```

The Output is

BCS

Physics

Chemistry

Maths 1

Maths2

Drawing

Bold tag

This tag is used to display the given text in bold letters. The general form is

```
<B>
Text to be displayed
</B>
```

Example

```
<B> My first HTML document </B>
```

The output is

My first HTML document

Italics tag

This tag is used to display the given text in italic. The general form is:

```
<I>
Text to be displayed
</I>
```

Example

```
<I> My first HTML document </l>
```

The output is

My first HTML document

Underline Tag

This tag is used to underline the given text. The general form is

```
<U>
Text to be displayed
</U>
```

Example

```
<U> My first HTML document </U>
```

The output is <u>My first HTML document</u>

Paragraph tag

This tag is used to begin a new paragraph. The general form is

```
<P attribute = "VALUE">
Text to be displayed
</P>
```

The closing tag </P> is optional. This has only one attribute namely ALIGN.

The different values are:

ALIGN="LEFT" – this aligns the following paragraph to left. This is the default alignment.

ALIGN="RIGHT"-this align the following paragraph to right.

ALIGN="CENTER"-this align the following paragraph to center.

ALIGN="JUSTIFY"-this justifies the following paragraph.

Example

<BODY>

My name is Ramu. I am studying in XYZ POLYTECHNIC. My father is a teacher <P> My interesting subject is BCS.

</BODY>

The output is

My name is Ramu. I am studying in XYZ POLYTECHNIC

My Father is a teacher.

My interesting subject is BCS.

BR tag

This tag is used to break the text following the <BR> and brought it to the next line. This has no closing tag. This general form is

Text to break

Example

(i) Without <BR> tag

<BODY> I am an <B> Indian </B>

I am proud of my country

</BODY>

The output is

I am an Indian I am proud of my country

(ii) With <BR> tag

<BODY> Iam an <B> Indian </B>

I am proud of my country

</BODY>

The output is

I am an Indian

I am proud of my country

HR tag

This tag is used to draw a horizontal line from left to right. This has no closing tag. The general form is

```
<HR>
```

Example

```
<BODY>
Basics of Computer Science
<HR> By EDWIN SELVA
</BODY>
```

The output is

Basics of computer science

By EDWIN SELVA

Font tag

This tag is used to specify the size of the font and colour of the text to be displayed. The general form is

```
<FONT attribute = "VALUE">
----------------------</FONT>
```

The attributes are

a) COLOR

This attribute is used to set a specific COLOR to the text within the tags. It can take values as red, green etc.

b) FACE

This attribute is used to set the type of the font to the text within the tags. It can take values as Arial, Roman etc.

c) SIZE

This attribute is used to set font size to the text within the tags. It can take values between 1 to 7.

Example

1) <FONT COLOUR="Blue">XYZ POLYTECHNIC </FONT> XYZ POLYTECHNIC will be displayed in blue color.

2) <FONT FACE="Arial">XYZ POLYTECHNIC </FONT> XYZ POLYTECHNIC will be displayed in arial font.

3) <FONT SIZE="7">XYZ POLYTECHNIC </FONT> XYZ POLYTECHNIC will be displayed in maximum size.

Strike Through

Strike through means, to draw a line over the middle of the text. For this <STRIKE> or <S> tag is used. This general form is

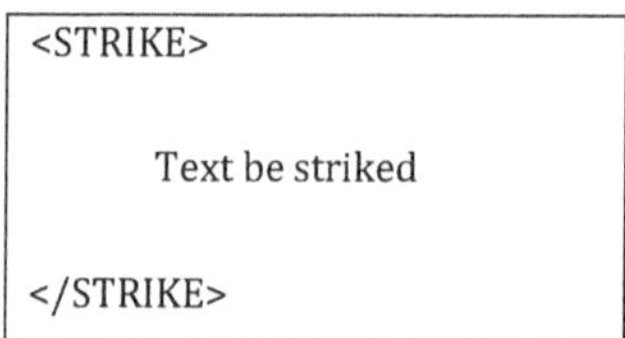

```
<STRIKE>

      Text be striked

</STRIKE>
```

Example

```
<STRIKE>
He is good
</STRIKE>
```

The output is

He is good

EM tag

This tag is used to give importance (emphasize) to portion of a text or full text. The general form is

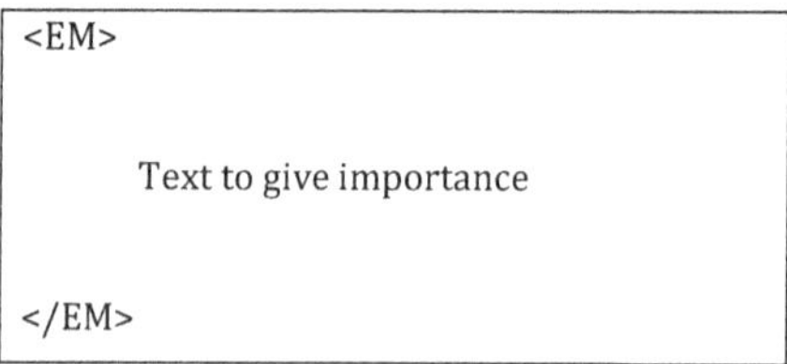

```
<EM>

      Text to give importance

</EM>
```

Example

<EM> god is love </EM>.

The output is god is love.

TT tag

This tag is used to display the enclosed text in teletype font. That is the text will be mono spaced to look like a typewriter font. The general form is

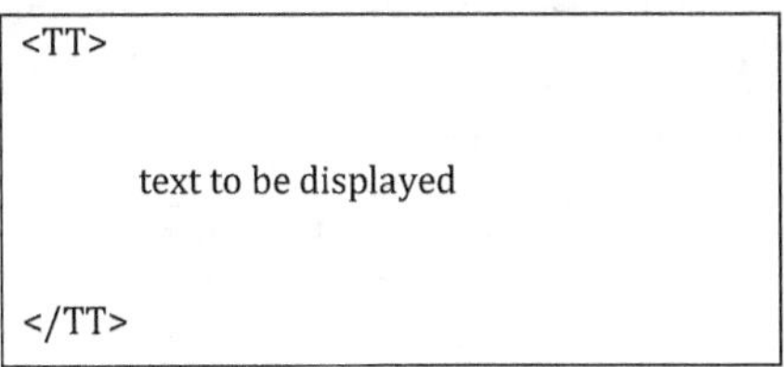

Example

<TT> God is love </TT>

PRE tag

This tag is used to preserve the line breaks and horizontal spacing in our text. The general form is

Example

<PRE>
God is love
So love god
</PRE>

The output is

God is love

So love god

Special Characters

Special characters are symbols used to give meaning to the following.

1) &, (ampersand), "(quotes), < > (angle brackets) are all reserved characters in html. So these characters cannot be used in our program. For using these characters in our

program special characters are available in html go give meaning to the reserved characters.

2) Special characters are available in html to substitute characters which are not available in our keyboard (foreign language characters). So we can use foreign language characters in our program.

The following table lists some special characters.

Character	Special character
"	&quoat;
<	<
>	>
&	&
Σ	σ
α	α
β	β

Example

```
<HTML>
<BODY>
& alpha;- ALPHA
</BODY>
</HTML>
```

The Output is

-ALPHA

Working with Images

<IMG> tag is used to add images in our document. This tag has no closing tag. The general form is

<IMG attribute = "VALUE">

The attributes are:

1) SRC : This attribute is used to give the name of the image file from where the image is to be loaded. The format of the file must be in GIF or JPEG.

2) WIDTH : This attribute is used to set the width of the image in pixels.

3) HEIGHT : This attribute is used to set the height of the image in pixels.

4) ALIGN : This attribute is used to align the picture. By default it is aligned to left.

5) ALT : This attribute is used to display and alternate message when the browser cannot display the images or if downloading the image takes long time.

6) HSPACE : This attribute is used to set the horizontal space between the text and image border.

7) VSPACE : This attribute is used to set the vertical space between the text and image border.

Example

<IMG SRC = "a.gif" ALT = "picture of a baby" ALIGN = 'RIGHT'>

META tag

This tag is used to define the information about the document itself. The important information to be defined are:

1) Name of the document generated software.
2) Keywords used in the document.
3) Details about the author of the document.
4) To get details about the date of modification of our document from the server.

Meta tag is included in the head tag and it has no closing tag. The general form is

<META NAME or HTTP-EQUIV="VALUE" CONTENT="VALUE">

The attributes are

1) NAME : This attribute is used to give the details about the author, software used, keywords etc.

2) HTTP-EQIV : This attribute is used to get information from the server.

3) CONTENT : This attribute is used to store this content of the attribute NAME and HTTP-EQIV

Example

1) <META NAME = "Author" CONTENT = "RAMKUMAR">
2) <META NAME = "KEYWORDS" CONTENT = "birds, restaurants, books">
3) <META HTTP-EQUIV= "Expires" CONTENT = "WED 2 OCT 2008 7:30: GMT">

2.2.   Advanced HTML

Links

Link is defined as a relationship between two documents or URLs. We can create two types of links between documents or URL's.

They are

1) Theoretical link using LINK.

2) Hyper link using another tag.

1) *Theoretical Link Using LINK tag*

To create links between documents <LINK> tag is used. The general form is

<LINK REL or REV = "relationship name"

HREF = "name of the document">

Where

REL : This attribute indicates the normal relationship with the document specified in the attribute HREF by the current document.

REV : This attribute indicates the relationship by the document specified in the attribute HREF with the current document.

This tag has no closing tag and is included within the head tag. This is used to indicate the theoretical relationship to other documents. This helps the browsers are search engines to know about the documents.

Let us consider the following two documents in a polytechnic website.

1) History.html – this contains the history of the polytechnic and it is a part of the web site.

2) Index.html – this contains the main or home page of the site.

   To make a theoretical relationship between these two documents, the following entries must be made using LINK tag in both documents

   History.html-<LINK REL = "index" HREF = "index.html">

   This helps the browser and search engine to know where they can find the home page.

   Index.html-<LINK REV = "index" HREF = "history.html">

   This helps the browser and search engine to know that there is a two-way relationship between history. Html and index.html.

3) Hyper Links Using Anchor Tag

   Anchor tag A is used to create internal and external link between documents. The linked documents can be accessed by anyone from anywhere in the world. The general form is

<A HREF = "file" TARGET = "value">
   Text
</A>

Where

HREF : this attribute is used to give the linkiing file name.

File : name of the file or URL to be linked.

Text : highlighted link part to be clicked. Usually this will be displayed in blue colour.

TARGET : this attribute value is used to target one frame from another.

When the high lighted portion of the link part in the document is clicked, the file specified in the HREF or frame specification TARGET is linked and will be opened.

Example

(i) To create a HTML page saved as main.html containing college name xyz and to link this page with another page saved as course.html, which contains course information. The link part in the first page is course.

Step -1 Create main.html

```
<HTML>
<HEAD>
<TITLE> POLYTECHNIC </TITLE>
</HEAD>
<BODY> xyz POLYTECHNIC
<A HREF = "course.html">
COURSE
</A>
</BODY>
</HTML>
```

Step 2 Create course.html

```
<HTML>
<HEAD>
<TITLE> COURSE OFFERED </TITLE>
</HEAD>
<BODY>
<H1> COURSES </H1>
<HR>
<OL>
<LI>CIVIL
<LI>MECHANICAL
```

<LI>COMPUTER

</OL>

</BODY>

</HTML>

Step -3 Open the document main.html in the internet explorer. The following page appears.

Xyz POLYTECHNIC <u>COURSE</u>

Step-4 Click COURSE in the page. Now, course.html page is linked and opened as shown below.

1.	CIVIL
2.	MECHANICAL
3.	COMPUTER

Lists

Lists are used to display information sequentially in a HTML page. Lists are divided into three types. They are:

1) Ordered list.
2) Un-ordered list.
3) Definition list.

1) Ordered List

In an ordered list, the information are numbered by any one of the following:

1) Number 1,2,3,.......
2) Upper case alphabets A,B,C.......
3) Lower case alphabets a,b,c......
4) Upper case Roman numbers I,II,III....
5) Lower case Roman numbers i,ii,iii

The ordered lists are created using <OL>........</OL> tags. The general form is

```
<OL TYPE = "VALUE1" START = "VALUE2">

<LI> Item -1--------------

<LI> Item -2--------------

    .

    .

    .

<LI> Item -n--------------

</LI>
```

Where

<Ll> - tag used to give the items in the list closing tag is optional.

TYPE, START – attribute.

VALUE1 – 1 or a or A or i or I.

VALUE2- start number of the ordered list.

Item 1, item 2…..item n – list of information.

Note: If attributes are not given, the default is numbers.

Example

1) <OL>

<Ll> CIVIL

<Ll> MECHANICAL

<Ll> INFORMATION TECHNOLOGY

</OL>

The output will be:

1) CIVIL

2) MECHANICAL

3) INFORMATION TECHNOLOGY

2) <OL TYPE = "1" START = "4">

<Ll> CIVIL

<Ll> MECHANICAL

<Ll> INFORMATION TECHNOLOGY

</OL>

The output will be

4) CIVIL

5) MECHANICAL

6) INFORMATION TECHNOLOGY

3) <OL TYPE = "I" START = "I">

<LI> ABC POLYTECHNIC

<OL TYPE = "a" START = "a">

<Ll> CIVIL

<Ll> MECHANICAL

</OL>

```
<LI> xyz POLYTECHNIC
<OL TYPE = "i" START = "i">
 <Li> COMPUTER TECHNOLOGY
<Li>INFORMATION TECHNOLOGY
<Li>ELECTRONICS
</OL>
</OL>
```

The output will be

I.   *ABC Polytechnic*

   1) CIVIL
   2) MECHANICAL

II.   *XYZ Polytechnic*

   1) COMPUTER TECHNOLOGY
   2) INFORMATION TECHNOLOGY
   3) ELECTRONICS

2) Un-Ordered List

In an un-ordered list, the information are preceded by any one of the following bullets.

   1) Circle
   2) Disc
   3) Square

The un-ordered lists are created using <UL>.......</UL>

HTML Example

A small HTML document

```
<!DOCTYPE html>
<html>
<head>
<title>Page Title</title>
</head>
<body>

<h1>My First Heading</h1>
<p>My first paragraph.</p>
```

```html
</body>
</html>
```

Example Explained

1) The **DOCTYPE** declaration defines the document type to be HTML
2) The text between **<html>** and **</html>** describes an HTML document
3) The text between **<head>** and **</head>** provides information about the document
4) The text between **<title>** and **</title>** provides a title for the document
5) The text between **<body>** and **</body>** describes the visible page content
6) The text between **<h1>** and **</h1>** describes a heading
7) The text between **<p>** and **</p>** describes a paragraph

Using this description, a web browser can display a document with a heading and a paragraph.

HTML Tags

1) HTML tags are **keywords** (tag names) surrounded by **angle brackets**:

<tagname>content</tagname>

1) HTML tags normally come **in pairs** like <p> and </p>
2) The first tag in a pair is the **start tag,** the second tag is the **end tag**
3) The end tag is written like the start tag, but with a **slash** before the tag name

Web Browsers

The purpose of a web browser (Chrome, IE, Firefox, Safari) is to read HTML documents and display them.

The browser does not display the HTML tags, but uses them to determine how to display the document:

HTML Page Structure

Below is a visualization of an HTML page structure:

<html>

<head>

<title>Page title</title>

</head>

<body>

<h1>This is a heading</h1>

<p>This is a paragraph.</p>

<p>This is another paragraph.</p>

</body>

</html>

The <!DOCTYPE> Declaration

The <!DOCTYPE> declaration helps the browser to display a web page correctly.

There are different document types on the web.

To display a document correctly, the browser must know both type and version.

The doctype declaration is not case sensitive. All cases are acceptable:

<!DOCTYPE html>

<!DOCTYPE HTML>

<!doctype html>

<!Doctype Html>

Common Declarations

HTML5
<!DOCTYPE html>
HTML 4.01
<!DOCTYPE HTML PUBLIC "-//W3C//DTD HTML 4.01 Transitional//EN"
"http://www.w3.org/TR/html4/loose.dtd">
XHTML 1.0
<!DOCTYPE html PUBLIC "-//W3C//DTD XHTML 1.0 Transitional//EN"
"http://www.w3.org/TR/xhtml1/DTD/xhtml1-transitional.dtd">

HTML Versions

Since the early days of the web, there have been many versions of HTML:

Version	Year
HTML	1991
HTML 2.0	1995
HTML 3.2	1997
HTML 4.01	1999
XHTML	2000
HTML5	2014

Write HTML Using Notepad or Text Edit

HTML can be edited by using professional HTML editors like:

1) Microsoft Web Matrix.

2) Sublime Text.

However, for learning HTML we recommend a text editor like Notepad (PC) or Text Edit (Mac).

We believe using a simple text editor is a good way to learn HTML.

Follow the 4 steps below to create your first web page with Notepad.

Step 1: Open Notepad

To open Notepad in Windows 7 or earlier:

Click Start (bottom left on your screen).

Click All Programs. Click Accessories. Click Notepad.

To open Notepad in Windows 8 or later:

Open the Start Screen (the window symbol at the bottom left on your screen). Type Notepad.

Step 2: Write Some HTML

Write or copy some HTML into Notepad.

```
<!DOCTYPE html>
<html>
<body>

<h1>My First Heading</h1>

<p>My first paragraph.</p>
```

```
</body>
</html>
```

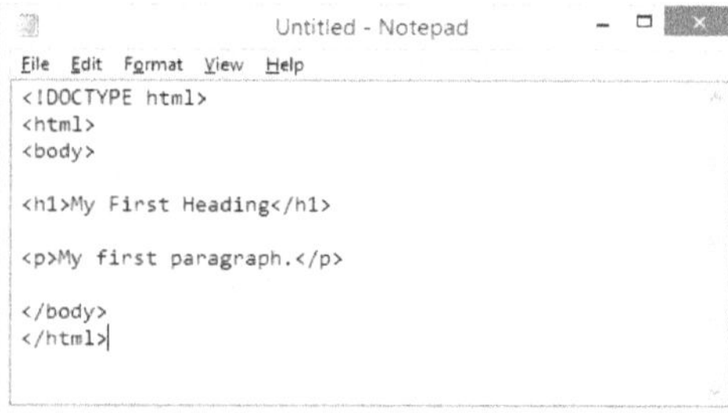

Step 3: Save the HTML Page

Save the file on your computer.

Select **File > Save as** in the Notepad menu.

Name the file "index.html" or any other name ending with html or htm.

UTF-8 is the preferred encoding for HTML files.

ANSI encoding covers US and Western European characters only.

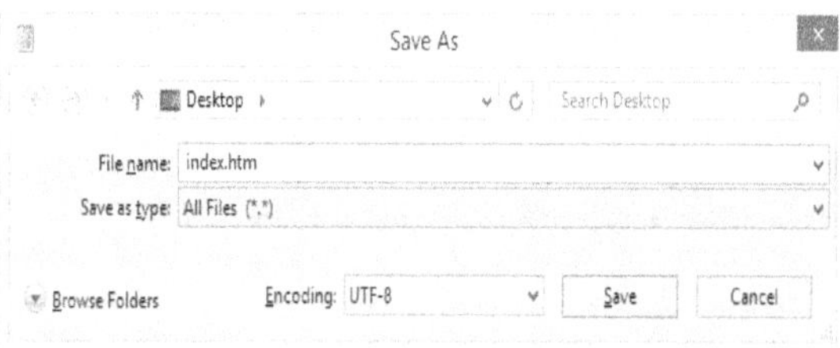

Step 4: View HTML Page in Your Browser

Open the saved HTML file in your favourite browser. The result will look much like this:

HTML Documents

All HTML documents must start with a type declaration: **<!DOCTYPE html>**.

The HTML document itself begins with **<html>** and ends with **</html>**.

The visible part of the HTML document is between **<body>** and **</body>**.

Example

```
<!DOCTYPE html>
<html>
<body>

<h1>My First Heading</h1>
<p>My first paragraph.</p>

</body>
</html>
```

HTML Headings

HTML headings are defined with the **<h1>** to **<h6>** tags:

Example

```
<h1>This is a heading</h1>
<h2>This is a heading</h2>
<h3>This is a heading</h3>
```

HTML Paragraphs

HTML paragraphs are defined with the **<p>** tag:

Example

```
<p>This is a paragraph.</p>
<p>This is another paragraph.</p>
```

HTML Links

HTML links are defined with the **<a>** tag:

Example

```
<a href="http://www.w3schools.com">This is a link</a>
```

The link's destination is specified in the **href attribute**.

Attributes are used to provide additional information about HTML elements.

HTML Images

HTML images are defined with the **<img>** tag.

The source file (**src**), alternative text (**alt**), and size (**width** and **height**) are provided as **attributes**:

Example

```
<img src="w3schools.jpg" alt="W3Schools.com" width="104" height="142">
```

HTML Elements

HTML elements are written with a **start** tag, with an **end** tag, with the **content** in between:

```
<tagname>content</tagname>
```

The HTML **element** is everything from the start tag to the end tag:

```
<p>My first HTML paragraph.</p>
```

Start tag	Element Content	End tag
<h1>	My First Heading	</h1>
<p>	My first paragraph.	</p>

Nested HTML Elements

HTML elements can be nested (elements can contain elements).

All HTML documents consist of nested HTML elements.

This example contains 4 HTML elements:

Example

```
<!DOCTYPE html>
<html>
<body>

<h1>My First Heading</h1>
<p>My first paragraph.</p>

</body>
</html>
```

HTML Example Explained

The **<html>** element defines the **whole document**.

It has a **start** tag <html> and an **end** tag </html>.

The element **content** is another HTML element (the <body> element).

<html>
<body>

<h1>My First Heading</h1>
<p>My first paragraph.</p>
</body>
</html>

The **<body>** element defines the **document body**.

It has a **start** tag <body> and an **end** tag </body>.

The element **content** is two other HTML elements (<h1> and <p>).

<body>

<h1>My First Heading</h1>
<p>My first paragraph.</p>

</body>

The **<h1>** element defines a **heading**.

It has a **start** tag <h1> and an **end** tag </h1>.

The element **content** is: My First Heading.

<h1>My First Heading</h1>

The **<p>** element defines a **paragraph**.

It has a **start** tag <p> and an **end** tag </p>.

The element **content** is: My first paragraph.

<p>My first paragraph.</p>

Don't Forget the End Tag

Some HTML elements will display correctly, even if you forget the end tag:

Example

<html>

<body>

<p>This is a paragraph

<p>This is a paragraph

</body>

</html>

The example above works in all browsers, because the closing tag is considered optional.

Never rely on this. It might produce unexpected results and/or errors if you forget the end tag.

Empty HTML Elements

HTML elements with no content are called empty elements.

 is an empty element without a closing tag (the <br> tag defines a line break).

Empty elements can be "closed" in the opening tag like this: <br />.

HTML5 does not require empty elements to be closed. But if you want stricter validation, or you need to make your document readable by XML parsers, you should close all HTML elements.

HTML Tip: Use Lowercase Tags

HTML tags are not case sensitive: <P> means the same as <p>.

The HTML5 standard does not require lowercase tags, but W3C **recommends** lowercase in HTML4, and **demands** lowercase for stricter document types like XHTML.

HTML Attributes

Attributes provide additional information about HTML elements.

HTML Attributes

1) HTML elements can have **attributes**
2) Attributes provide **additional information** about an element
3) Attributes are always specified in **the start tag**
4) Attributes come in name/value pairs like: **name="value"**

The Lang Attribute

The document language can be declared in the **<html>** tag.

The language is declared in the **lang** attribute.

Declaring a language is important for accessibility applications (screen readers) and search engines:

```
<!DOCTYPE html>
<html lang="en-US">
<body>
<h1>My First Heading</h1>
<p>My first paragraph.</p>


</body>
</html>
```

The first two letters specify the language (en). If there is a dialect, use two more letters (US).

The Title Attribute

HTML paragraphs are defined with the **<p>** tag.

In this example, the **<p>** element has a **title** attribute. The value of the attribute is "**About W3Schools**":

Example

```
<p title="AboutW3Schools">
```

W3Schools is a web developer's site. It provides tutorials and references covering many aspects of web programming, including HTML, CSS, JavaScript, XML, SQL, PHP, ASP, etc.

```
</p>
```

The href Attribute

HTML links are defined with the **<a>** tag.

The link address is specified in the **href** attribute:

Example

```
<a href="http://www.w3schools.com">This is a link</a>
```

You will learn more about links and the <a> tag later in this tutorial.

Size Attributes

HTML images are defined with the **<img>** tag.

The filename of the source (**src**), and the size of the image (**width** and **height**) are all provided as **attributes**.

Example

<img src="w3schools.jpg" width="104" height="142">

The image size is specified in pixels: width="104" means 104 screen pixels wide.

You will learn more about images and the <img> tag later in this tutorial.

The Alt Attribute

The **alt** attribute specifies an alternative text to be used, when an HTML element cannot be displayed.

The value of the attribute can be read by "screen readers". This way, someone "listening" to the webpage, i.e. a blind person, can "hear" the element.

Example

<img src="w3schools.jpg" alt="W3Schools.com" width="104" height="142">

We Suggest: Always Use Lowercase Attributes

The HTML5 standard does not require lower case attribute names.

The title attribute can be written with upper or lower case like **Title** and/or **TITLE**.

W3C **recommends** lowercase in HTML4, and **demands** lowercase for stricter document types like XHTML.

We Suggest: Always Quote Attribute Values

The HTML5 standard does not require quotes around attribute values.

The **href** attribute, demonstrated above, can be written as:

Example

<a href=http://www.w3schools.com>

W3C **recommends** quotes in HTML4, and **demands** quotes for stricter document types like XHTML.

Sometimes it is **necessary** to use quotes.

This will not display correctly, because it contains a space:

Example

```
<p title=About W3Schools>
```

Single or Double Quotes?

Double style quotes are the most common in HTML, but single style can also be used.

In some situations, when the attribute value itself contains double quotes, it is necessary to use single quotes:

```
<p title='John "ShotGun" Nelson'>
```

Or vice versa:

```
<p title="John 'ShotGun' Nelson">
```

Headings are important in HTML documents.

HTML Headings

Headings are defined with the <h1> to <h6> tags.

<h1> defines the most important heading. <h6> defines the least important heading.

Example

```
<h1>This is a heading</h1>
<h2>This is a heading</h2>
<h3>This is a heading</h3>
```

Note

Browsers automatically add some empty space (a margin) before and after each heading.

Headings Are Important

Use HTML headings for headings only. Don't use headings to make text **BIG** or **bold**.

Search engines use your headings to index the structure and content of your web pages.

Users skim your pages by its headings.

It is important to use headings to show the document structure.

h1 headings should be main headings, followed by h2 headings, then the less important h3, and so on.

HTML Horizontal Rules

The **<hr>** tag creates a horizontal line in an HTML page.

The hr element can be used to separate content:

Example

```
<p>This is a paragraph.</p>
<hr>
<p>This is a paragraph.</p>
<hr>
<p>This is a paragraph.</p>
```

The HTML <head> Element

The HTML **<head>** element has nothing to do with HTML headings.

The HTML <head> element contains **meta data**. Meta data are not displayed.

The HTML <head> element is placed between the <html> tag and the <body> tag:

Example

```
<!DOCTYPE html>
<html>

<head>
 <title>My First HTML</title>
 <meta charset="UTF-8">
</head>

<body>
 .

 .

 .

HTML Paragraphs
```

HTML documents are divided into paragraphs.

HTML Paragraphs

The HTML **<p>** element defines a **paragraph**.

Example

```
<p>This is a paragraph</p>
<p>This is another paragraph</p>
```

HTML Display

You cannot be sure how HTML will be displayed.

Large or small screens, and resized windows will create different results.

With HTML, you cannot change the output by adding extra spaces or extra lines in your HTML code.

The browser will remove extra spaces and extra lines when the page is displayed.

Any number of spaces, and any number of new lines, counts as **only one space**.

Example

```
<p>
This paragraph
contains a lot of lines
in the source code,
but the browser
ignores it.
</p>

<p>
This paragraph
contains        a lot of spaces
in the source            code,
but the          browser
ignores it.
</p>
```

Most browsers will display HTML correctly even if you forget the end tag:

Example

```
<p>This is a paragraph
<p>This is another paragraph
```

The example above will work in most browsers, but do not rely on it.

Forgetting the end tag can produce unexpected results or errors.

HTML Line Breaks

The HTML **
** element defines a **line break**.

Use <br> if you want a line break (a new line) without starting a new paragraph:

Example

This is
a para
graph with line breaks

The <br> element is an empty HTML element. It has no end tag.

The Poem Problem

Example

This poem will display as one line:

  My Bonnie lies over the ocean.

  My Bonnie lies over the sea.

  My Bonnie lies over the ocean.

  Oh, bring back my Bonnie to me.

The HTML <pre> Element

The HTML <pre> element defines preformatted text.

The text inside a <pre> element is displayed in a fixed-width font (usually Courier), and it preserves both spaces and line breaks:

Example

<pre>

  My Bonnie lies over the ocean.

  My Bonnie lies over the sea.

  My Bonnie lies over the ocean.

  Oh, bring back my Bonnie to me.

</pre>

The HTML <title> Element

The HTML **<title>** element is meta data. It defines the HTML document's title.

The title will not be displayed in the document, but might be displayed in the browser tab.

The HTML <meta> Element

The HTML **<meta>** element is also meta data.

It can be used to define the character set, and other information about the HTML document.

More Meta Elements

In the chapter about HTML styles you discover more meta elements:

The HTML **<style>** element is used to define internal CSS style sheets.

The HTML **<link>** element is used to define external CSS style sheets.

HTML Tip - How to View HTML Source.

Have you ever seen a Web page and wondered "Hey! How did they do that?"

To find out, right-click in the page and select "View Page Source" (in Chrome) or "View Source" (in IE), or similar in another browser.

This will open a window containing the HTML code of the page.

HTML Styles

I am red

I am blue

The HTML Style Attribute

Setting the style of an HTML element, can be done with the **style attribute**.

The HTML style attribute has the following **syntax**:

$$style="property:value;"$$

The *property* is a CSS property. The *value* is a CSS value.

HTML Background Color

The **background-color** property defines the background color for an HTML element:

This example sets the background for a page to lightgrey:

Example

```
<body style="background-color:lightgrey;">

<h1>This is a heading</h1>
<p>This is a paragraph.</p>


</body>
```

HTML Text Color

The **color** property defines the text color for an HTML element:

Example

```
<h1 style="color:blue;">This is a heading</h1>
<p style="color:red;">This is a paragraph.</p>
```

HTML Fonts

The **font-family** property defines the font to be used for an HTML element:

Example

```
<h1 style="font-family:verdana;">This is a heading</h1>
<p style="font-family:courier;">This is a paragraph.</p>
```

HTML Text Size

The **font-size** property defines the text size for an HTML element:

Example

```
<h1 style="font-size:300%;">This is a heading</h1>
<p style="font-size:160%;">This is a paragraph.</p>
```

HTML Text Alignment

The **text-align** property defines the horizontal text alignment for an HTML element:

Example

```
<h1 style="text-align:center;">Centered Heading</h1>
<p>This is a paragraph.</p>
```

T

HTML Text Formatting Elements

Text Formatting

This text is bold

This text is italic

This is superscript

HTML Formatting Elements

In the previous chapter, you learned about HTML **styling**, using the HTML **style attribute**.

HTML also defines special **elements** for defining text with a special **meaning**.

HTML uses elements like <b> and <i> for formatting output, like **bold** or *italic* text.

Formatting elements were designed to display special **types of text**:

1) Bold text.
2) Important text.
3) Italic text.
4) Emphasized text.
5) Marked text.
6) Small text.
7) Deleted text.
8) Inserted text.
9) Subscripts.
10) Superscripts.

HTML Bold and Strong Formatting

The HTML **<b>** element defines **bold** text, without any extra importance.

Example

```
<p>This text is normal.</p>
<p><b>This text is bold</b>.</p>
```

The HTML **<strong>** element defines **strong** text, with added semantic "strong" importance.

Example

```
<p>This text is normal.</p>
<p><strong>This text is strong</strong>.</p>
```

HTML Italic and Emphasized Formatting

The HTML **<i>** element defines *italic* text, without any extra importance.

Example

```
<p>This text is normal.</p>

<p><i>This text is italic</i>.</p>
```

The HTML **<em>** element defines *emphasized* text, with added semantic importance.

Example

```
<p>This text is normal.</p>

<p><em>This text is emphasized</em>.</p>
```

> Browsers display <strong> as <b>, and <em> as <i>.
> However, there is a difference in the meaning of these tags: <b> and <i> defines bold and italic text, but <strong> and <em> means that the text is "important".

HTML Small Formatting

The HTML **<small>** element defines **small** text:

Example

```
<h2>HTML <small>Small</small> Formatting</h2>
```

HTML Marked Formatting

The HTML **<mark>** element defines **marked** or highlighted text:

Example

```
<h2>HTML <mark>Marked</mark> Formatting</h2>
```

Try it Yourself »

HTML Deleted Formatting

The HTML **<del>** element defines **deleted** (removed) text.

Example

```
<p>My favorite color is <del>blue</del> red.</p>
```

HTML Inserted Formatting

The HTML **<ins>** element defines **inserted** (added) text.

Example

```
<p>My favorite <ins>color</ins> is red.</p>
```

HTML Subscript Formatting

The HTML **<sub>** element defines **subscripted** text.

Example

    This is _{subscripted} text.

HTML Superscript Formatting

The HTML **<sup>** element defines **superscripted** text.

Example

    This is ^{superscripted} text.

HTML Quotation and Citation Elements

Quotation

Here is a quote from WWF's website:

For 50 years, WWF has been protecting the future of nature. The world's leading conservation organization, WWF works in 100 countries and is supported by 1.2 million members in the United States and close to 5 million globally.

HTML <q> for Short Quotations

The HTML **<q>** element defines a short quotation.

Browsers usually insert quotation marks around the <q> element.

Example

<p>WWF's goal is to: <q>Build a future where people live in harmony with nature.</q></p>

    HTML <blockquote> for Long Quotations

    The HTML **<blockquote>** element defines a quoted section.

    Browsers usually indent <blockquote> elements.

Example

    Here is a quote from WWF's website:
    <blockquote cite="http://www.worldwildlife.org/who/index.html">
    For 50 years, WWF has been protecting the future of nature.
    The world's leading conservation organization,
    WWF works in 100 countries and is supported by
    1.2 million members in the United States and
    close to 5 million globally.
    </blockquote>

HTML *<abbr> for Abbreviations*

The HTML **<abbr>** element defines an abbreviation or an acronym.

Marking abbreviations can give useful information to browsers, translation systems and search-engines.

Example

<p>The <abbr title="World Health Organization">WHO</abbr> was founded in 1948.</p>

HTML *<address> for Contact Information*

The HTML **<address>** element defines contact information (author/owner) of a document or article.

The <address> element is usually displayed in italic. Most browsers will add a line break before and after the element.

Example

<address>
Written by Jon Doe.
Visit us at:
Example.com
Box 564, Disneyland
USA
</address>

HTML *<cite> for Work Title*

The HTML **<cite>** element defines the title of a work.

Browsers usually display <cite> elements in italic.

Example

<p><cite>The Scream</cite> by Edward Munch. Painted in 1893.</p>
HTML <bdo> for Bi-Directional Override.
The HTML **<bdo>** element defines bi-directional override.
The <bdo> element is used to override the current text direction.

Example

<bdo dir="rtl">This text will be written from right to left</bdo>

Computer Code Element

```
<code>
var x = 5;
var y = 6;
document.getElementById("demo").innerHTML = x + y;
</code>
```

HTML Computer Code Formatting

HTML normally uses variable letter size and spacing.

This is not wanted when displaying examples of computer code.

The **<kbd>**, **<samp>**, and **<code>** elements all support fixed letter size and spacing.

HTML <kbd> For Keyboard Input

The HTML **<kbd>** element defines keyboard input:

Example

```
<kbd>File | Open...</kbd>
```

Result

File | Open...

HTML <samp> For Computer Output

The HTML **<samp>** element defines sample output from a computer program:

Example

```
<samp>
demo.example.com login: Apr 12 09:10:17
Linux 2.6.10-grsec+gg3+e+fhs6b+nfs+gr0501+++p3+c4a+gr2b-reslog-v6.189
</samp>
```

Result

demo.example.com login: Apr 12 09:10:17 Linux 2.6.10-grsec+gg3+e+fhs6b+nfs+gr0501+++p3+c4a+gr2b-reslog-v6.189

HTML <code> For Computer Code

The HTML **<code>** element defines a piece of programming code:

Example

```
<code>
var x = 5;
var y = 6;
document.getElementById("demo").innerHTML = x + y;
</code>
```

Result

var x = 5; var y = 6; document.getElementById("demo").innerHTML = x + y;

Notice that the <code> element does not preserve extra whitespace and line-breaks.

To fix this, you can put the <code> element inside a **<pre>** element:

Example

```
<pre>
<code>
var x = 5;
var y = 6;
document.getElementById("demo").innerHTML = x + y;
</code>
</pre>
```

Result

```
var x = 5;
var y = 6;
document.getElementById("demo").innerHTML = x + y;
```

HTML <var> For Variables

The HTML **<var>** element defines a variable.

The variable could be a variable in a mathematical expression or a variable in programming context:

Example

Einstein wrote: <var>E</var> = <var>m</var><var>c</var>².

Result

Einstein wrote: $E = mc^2$.

HTML Comments

Comment tags <!-- and --> are used to insert comments in HTML.

HTML Comment Tags

You can add comments to your HTML source by using the following syntax:

<!-- Write your comments here -->

Comments are not displayed by the browser, but they can help document your HTML.

With comments you can place notifications and reminders in your HTML:

Example

<!-- This is a comment -->

<p>This is a paragraph.</p>

<!-- Remember to add more information here -->

Comments are also great for debugging HTML, because you can comment out HTML lines of code, one at a time, to search for errors:

Example

<!-- Do not display this at the moment

<img border="0" src="pic_mountain.jpg" alt="Mountain">

-->

Conditional Comments

You might stumble upon conditional comments in HTML:

<!--[if IE 8]>

.... some HTML here ....

<![endif]-->

Conditional comments defines HTML tags to be executed by Internet Explorer only.

Software Program Tags

HTML comments tags can also be generated by various HTML software programs.

For example <!--webbot bot--> tags wrapped inside HTML comments by FrontPage and Expression Web.

As a rule, let these tags stay, to help support the software that created them.

HTML Styles - CSS

CSS = Styles and Colors

M a n i p u l a t e   T e x t

C o l o r s ,   B o x e s

Styling HTML with CSS

CSS stands for **C**ascading **S**tyle **S**heets

Styling can be added to HTML elements in 3 ways:

1) Inline - using a **style attribute** in HTML elements
2) Internal - using a **<style> element** in the HTML <head> section
3) External - using one or more **external CSS files**

The most common way to add styling, is to keep the styles in separate CSS files. But, in this tutorial, we use internal styling, because it is easier to demonstrate, and easier for you to try it yourself.

Inline Styling (Inline CSS)

Inline styling is used to apply a unique style to a single HTML element:

Inline styling uses the **style** attribute.

This example changes the text color of the <h1> element to blue:

Example

```
<h1 style="color:blue;">This is a Blue Heading</h1>
```
Try it Yourself »

Internal Styling (Internal CSS)

Internal styling is used to define a style for one HTML page.

Internal styling is defined in the **<head>** section of an HTML page, within a **<style>** element:

Example

```
<!DOCTYPE html>
<html>
<head>
<style>
body {background-color:lightgrey;}
```

```
h1  {color:blue;}
p   {color:green;}
</style>
</head>
<body>

<h1>This is a heading</h1>
<p>This is a paragraph.</p>

</body>
</html>
```

External Styling (External CSS)

An external style sheet is used to define the style for many pages.

With an **external style sheet**, you can change the look of an entire web site by changing one file!

To use an external style sheet, add a link to it in the **<head>** section of the HTML page:

Example

```
<!DOCTYPE html>
<html>
<head>
  <link rel="stylesheet" href="styles.css">
</head>
<body>

<h1>This is a heading</h1>
<p>This is a paragraph.</p>

</body>
</html>
```

An external style sheet can be written in any text editor. The file should not contain any html tags. The style sheet file must be saved with a .css extension.

Here is how the "styles.css" looks:

```css
body {
    background-color: lightgrey;
}

h1 {
    color: blue;
}

p {
    color:green;
}
```

CSS Fonts

The CSS **color** property defines the text color to be used for the HTML element.

The CSS **font-family** property defines the font to be used for the HTML element.

The CSS **font-size** property defines the text size to be used for the HTML element.

Example

```html
<!DOCTYPE html>
<html>
<head>
<style>
h1 {
    color: blue;
    font-family: verdana;
    font-size: 300%;
}
p {
    color: red;
    font-family: courier;
    font-size: 160%;
}
</style>
</head>
```

```
<body>

<h1>This is a heading</h1>
<p>This is a paragraph.</p>

</body>
</html>
```

The CSS Box Model

Every HTML element has a box around it, even if you cannot see it.

The CSS **border** property defines a visible border around an HTML element:

Example

```
p {
   border: 1px solid black;
}
```

The CSS **padding** property defines a padding (space) inside the border:

Example

```
p {
   border: 1px solid black;
   padding: 10px;
}
```

The CSS **margin** property defines a margin (space) outside the border:

Example

```
p {
   border: 1px solid black;
   padding: 10px;
   margin: 30px;
}
```

The id Attribute

All the examples above use CSS to style HTML elements in a general way.

To define a special style for one special element, first add an id attribute to the element:

```
<p id="p01">I am different</p>
```

then define a different style for the (identified) element:

Example

```
p#p01 {
    color: blue;
}
```

The class Attribute

To define a style for a special type (class) of elements, add a class attribute to the element:

```
<p class="error">I am different</p>
```

Now you can define a different style for all elements with the specified class:

Example

```
p.error {
color: red;
}
```

HTML Links

Links are found in nearly all web pages. Links allow users to click their way from page to page.

HTML Links - Hyperlinks

HTML links are hyperlinks.

A hyperlink is a text or an image you can click on, and jump to another document.

HTML Links - Syntax

In HTML, links are defined with the **<a>** tag:

```
<a href="url">link text</a>
```

Example

```
<a href="http://www.w3schools.com/html/">Visit our HTML tutorial</a>
```

The **href** attribute specifies the destination address (http://www.w3schools.com/html/)

The **link text** is the visible part (Visit our HTML tutorial).

Clicking on the link text, will send you to the specified address.

Local Links

The example above used an absolute URL (A full web address). A local link (link to the same web site) is specified with a relative URL (without http://www....).

Example

```
<a href="html_images.asp">HTML Images</a>
```

HTML Links - Colors

When you move the mouse over a link, two things will normally happen:

1) The mouse arrow will turn into a little hand.
2) The color of the link element will change.

By default, a link will appear like this (in all browsers):

1) An unvisited link is underlined and blue.
2) A visited link is underlined and purple.
3) An active link is underlined and red.

You can change the default colors, by using styles:

Example

```
<style>
a:link   {color:green; background-color:transparent; text-decoration:none}
a:visited {color:pink; background-color:transparent; text-decoration:none}
a:hover   {color:red; background-color:transparent; text-decoration:underline}
a:active {color:yellow; background-color:transparent; text-decoration:underline}
</style>
```

HTML Links - The Target Attribute

The **target** attribute specifies where to open the linked document. This example will open the linked document in a new browser window or in a new tab:

Example

```
<a href="http://www.w3schools.com/" target="_blank">Visit W3Schools!</a>
```

Target Value	Description
_blank	Opens the linked document in a new window or tab
_self	Opens the linked document in the same frame as it was clicked (this is default)
_parent	Opens the linked document in the parent frame
_top	Opens the linked document in the full body of the window
framename	Opens the linked document in a named frame

If your webpage is locked in a frame, you can use target="_top" to break out of the frame:

Example

<a href="http://www.w3schools.com/html/" target="_top">HTML5 tutorial!</a>

HTML Links - Image as Link

It is common to use images as links

Example

<a href="default.asp">

<img src="smiley.gif" alt="HTML tutorial" style="width:42px;height:42px;border:0">

</a>

HTML Links - Create a Bookmark

HTML bookmarks are used to allow readers to jump to specific parts of a Web page.

Bookmarks are practical if your website has long pages.

To make a bookmark, you must first create the bookmark, and then add a link to it.

When the link is clicked, the page will scroll to the location with the bookmark.

Example

First, create a bookmark with the id attribute:

<h2 id="tips">Useful Tips Section</h2>

Then, add a link to the bookmark ("Useful Tips Section"), from within the same page:

<a href="#tips">Visit the Useful Tips Section</a>

Or, add a link to the bookmark ("Useful Tips Section"), from another page:

Example

<a href="html_tips.html#tips">Visit the Useful Tips Section</a>

HTML Links

Links are found in nearly all web pages. Links allow users to click their way from page to page.

HTML Links - Hyperlinks

A hyperlink is a text or an image you can click on, and jump to another document.

HTML Links - Syntax

In HTML, links are defined with the **<a>** tag: <a href="*url*">*link text*</a>

Example

```
<a href="http://www.w3schools.com/html/">Visit our HTML tutorial</a>
```

The **href** attribute specifies the destination address (http://www.w3schools.com/html/)

The **link text** is the visible part (Visit our HTML tutorial).

Clicking on the link text, will send you to the specified address.

Local Links

The example above used an absolute URL (A full web address).

A local link (link to the same web site) is specified with a relative URL (without http://www....).

Example

```
<a href="html_images.asp">HTML Images</a>
```

HTML Links-Colors

When you move the mouse over a link, two things will normally happen:

1) The mouse arrow will turn into a little hand
2) The color of the link element will change

By default, a link will appear like this (in all browsers):

1) An unvisited link is underlined and blue
2) A visited link is underlined and purple
3) An active link is underlined and red

You can change the default colors, by using styles:

Example

```
<style>
a:link   {color:green; background-color:transparent; text-decoration:none}
a:visited {color:pink; background-color:transparent; text-decoration:none}
a:hover  {color:red; background-color:transparent; text-decoration:underline}
a:active {color:yellow; background-color:transparent; text-decoration:underline}
</style>
```

HTML Links-The Target Attribute

The **target** attribute specifies where to open the linked document.

This example will open the linked document in a new browser window or in a new tab:

Example

```
<a href="http://www.w3schools.com/" target="_blank">Visit W3Schools!</a>
```

Target Value	Description
_blank	Opens the linked document in a new window or tab
_self	Opens the linked document in the same frame as it was clicked (this is default)
_parent	Opens the linked document in the parent frame
_top	Opens the linked document in the full body of the window
framename	Opens the linked document in a named frame

If your webpage is locked in a frame, you can use target="_top" to break out of the frame:

Example

```
<a href="http://www.w3schools.com/html/" target="_top">HTML5 tutorial!</a>
```

HTML Links - Image as Link

It is common to use images as links:

Example

```
<a href="default.asp">
  <img src="smiley.gif" alt="HTML tutorial" style="width:42px;height:42px;border:0">
</a>
```

HTML Links - Create a Bookmark

HTML bookmarks are used to allow readers to jump to specific parts of a Web page.

Bookmarks are practical if your website has long pages.

To make a bookmark, you must first create the bookmark, and then add a link to it.

When the link is clicked, the page will scroll to the location with the bookmark.

Example

First, create a bookmark with the id attribute:

```
<h2 id="tips">Useful Tips Section</h2>
```

Then, add a link to the bookmark ("Useful Tips Section"), from within the same page:

```
<a href="#tips">Visit the Useful Tips Section</a>
```

Or, add a link to the bookmark ("Useful Tips Section"), from another page:

Example

```
<a href="html_tips.html#tips">Visit the Useful Tips Section</a>
```

UNIT-III

JAVA SCRIPT BASIC

Java Script

It is scripting language used to enhance the functionality of web browser. It shares many of the features and structures of the full java language. It is integrated with HTML and web browser. It is a platform independent, even-driven, interpreted programming language. This is an interpreted based language or source code fills or directly executed at run time. It includes build-in objects such as math, string and date functions.

Java Script Basic

We can embed java script using the following tag. <script> tag specify the java script source using the script tag. Script tag is an extension of HTML that can enclose any number of java script statements.

Syntax

<script> Java script statements </script>

A document can have multiple script tags and each can enclose any number of script statements.

Specifying the Java Script Version

The optional language attribute specifies this scripting language and java script version.

Syntax

<script language = "java script version">

Java script statements

</script>

Hiding Scripts Within Comment Tags

To ensure that the other browsers ignore java script code place the entire script within html comment tags.

Syntax

<script>

<!.......... Begin to hide script contents from old browsers ....>

</script>

Document Write

It is used to print the text in the client window.

Document Writeln

It is used to attach the output text with a carriage writeln added at the end of the string being displayed work in <pre> tag.

Eg: (document write)

<html>

<body>

<script language = "javascript">

Document.write ("Good Morning");

</script>

</body>

</html>

Eg: (document.writeln)

<html>

<body>

<pre>

<script language = "javascript">

Document.writeln ("Happy Birthday");

Document.write ("To Meena");

</script>

</pre>

</body>

</html>

Variables

Variables are the container for storing values in access numbers and alphabets. A variable can change using the scripts execution.

Eg: var x = 20

Datatypes in Java Script

a) Numbers

It is an integer value. It may be +ve or –ve. It is expressed in decimal, hexadecimal and octal base.

b) String

Strings are enclosed within single or double quotation marks. It is used to access alphabets.

c) Boolean

It holds either true or false values.

d) Null

Null means nothing. It has no values.

Operators in Java Script

An operator is a symbol that tells the computer to perform certain mathematical or logical manipulations. Operators are used in program to manipulate data and variables. Operators can be classified into a number of categories:

1) Arithmetic Operator
2) Relational Operator
3) Logical Operator
4) Assignment Operator
5) Increment or Decrement Operator
6) Conditional Operator
7) Bitwise Operator
8) Special Operator

1. Arithmetic Operator

Arithmetic operators are used to construct mathematical expressions as in algebra. The operators +, -, *, / all work in the same way as they do in other languages.

Operator	Meaning
+	Addition or unary plus
-	Subtraction or unary minus
*	Multiplication
/	Division
%	Modulus division

2. Relational Operator

Relational operators are used to do comparison.

Operator	Meaning
<	Is less than
>	Is greater than
<=	Is less than or equal to
>=	Is greater than or equal to
==	Is equal to
!=	Is not equal to

3. Logical Operator

Logical operators are used to test more than one condition and make decision.

Operator	Meaning
&&	Logical AND
||	Logical OR
!	Logical NOT

4. Assignment Operator

Assignment operators are used to assign the result of an expression to a variable. The usual assignment operator is = (equal to)

Syntax

v op = exp;

Here v is a variable, exp is an expression and op is a operator.

Shorthand Operator

Syntax

v = v op(exp);

with v evaluated only once.

Eg: **x + = y + 1 same as x = x + (y + 1)**

Here "+ =" means 'add y + 1 to x' or increment 'x by y + 1'.

Statement with simple assignment operator	Statement with shorthand operator
a = a + 1	a + = 1
a = a – 1	a - = 1
a = a * (n + 1)	a * = n + 1
a = a / (n + 1)	a / = (n + 1)
a = a % b	a % = b

5. *Increment or Decrement Operator*

Increment operators are used to add 1 to the operands. Decrement operators are used to subtract 1 from the operands. It is classified into 2 types.

1) Post increment and decrement operators.

2) Pre increment and decrement operators.

Syntax: (Post Increment and Decrement Operator)

++m;

--m;

Syntax: (Pre Increment and Decrement Operator)

m++;

m--;

The prefix operator first adds 1 to the operands and then the result is assignment to the variable on the left. It is on the other hand, the postfix operator first assigns the value to the variable and then increment the operand.

6. *Conditional Operator*

Syntax

exp 1 ? exp 2 : exp 3

"?" – ternary operator exp 1, exp2, exp 3 – expressions.

Exp 1 is evaluated first. It is non zero then the exp 2 is evaluated and becomes the value of the expression.

If the exp1 is false, exp 3 is evaluated and its value becomes the value of the expression.

7. *Bitwise Operator*

Bitwise operators are used for manipulation of data at bit level. These operators are used for testing the bits or shifting them right or left. Bitwise operator may not be applied to float or double.

Operator	Meaning
&	Bitwise AND
|	Bitwise OR
^	Bitwise Exclusive OR
<<	Shift left
>>	Shift right

8. Special Operator

'comma', 'size of', 'pointer operator' (& and *), 'member selection operator' (. and →)

The Comma operator can be used to link the related expressions together. A comma linked list of expressions is evaluated left to right.

Example

value = (x = 10; y = 5; x + y);

The size of operator is compiled time operator and when used with an operand it returns the number of bytes the operand occupies. It is normally used to determine the length of the arrays and structures.

Java Script Statements

Control Statements

Control statements are designed to create scripts that can decide which lines of code are evaluated or how many times to evaluate them. There are two types of control statements. They are:

1) Conditional Statements.
2) Loop Statements.

1. Conditional Statements

If Statement

Syntax

If(test expression)

{

    Statement_block;

}

Statement_x;

The "statement_block" may be a single statement or group of statements. If the text expression is true, the statement_block will be executed otherwise the statement_block will be skipped and the execution will jumped into statement_x.

Eg: for If Statement

```
<html>
<head>
<title> If Statement </title>
</head>
<body>
<script language = "javascript">
var a = 20;
if(a >= 18)
                document.write("Eligible to vote");
</script>
</body>
</html>
```

If....Else Statement

The if....else statement is the extension of simple if statement.

Syntax

```
            If(test expression)
            {
                        True block statement(s);
            }
            Else
            {
                        False block statement(s);
            }
            Statement_x;
```

If the test expression is true, then the true block statement(s) immediately following the if statement are executed, otherwise false block statement(s) are executed. In either true or false will be executed and not both.

Eg for Conditional Operator

```
<html>
<head>
<title> Conditional Operator </title>
```

```
</head>
<body>
<script language = "javascript">
var a = 5, b = 6;
var x = a > b? a : b;
document.writeln(x);
</script>
</body>
</html>
```

Eg for if....Else Statement

```
<html>
<head>
<title> if...else statement </title>
</head>
<body>
<script language = "javascript">
var a = 10;
if(a % 2 == 0)
 document.write("Even Number");
else
document.write("Odd Number");
</script>
</body>
</html>
```

Eg for Postfix

```
<html>
<head>
<title> Postfix </title>
</head>
<body>
<script language = "javascript">
var i,j,n;
n = prompt("Enter n =");
```

```
for(i=1; i<=n; i++)
{
                document.writeln();
                for(j=1; j>=i; j--)
                document.write("*");
}
</script>
</body>
</html>
```

Eg for Conditional Operator

```
<html>
<head>
<title> Conditional Operator </title>
</head>
<body>
<script language = "javascript">
var a = 5, b = 6;
var x = a > b? a : b;
document.writeln(x);
</script>
</body>
</html>
```

Nested If Statement

Syntax

```
        if(test condition 1)
        {
                if(test condition 2)
                {
                        Statement 1;
                }
                else
                {
                        Statement 2;
```

                    }
        }
        else
        {
                Statement 3;
        }
Statement_x;

When a series of decision are involved we may have to use more than one if....else statement in nested form. If the condition 1 is false statement 3 will be executed. Otherwise it continues to perform the second test.

If the condition 2 is true statement 1 will be evaluated. Otherwise the statement 2 will be evaluated and then the control is transferred to statement x.

Eg

```
<html>
<head>
<title> Greatest Number </title>
</head>
<body>
<script language = "javascript">
var a = 10, b = 5, c = 3;
if(a > b && a > c)
        document.write("a is greater");
else if(b > c)
        document.write("b is greater");
else
        document.write("c is greater");
</script>
</body>
</html>
```

Switch Statement

Build –in multi way decision statement is known as switch. The switch statement tests the value of a given variable against a list of case values and when a match is found a block of statements associated with that case is executed.

Syntax

```
switch(expression)
{
            case value 1:
                        block_1;
                        break;
            case value 2:
                        break;
                        block_2;


            ................
            ................
            default:
                        default_block;
                        break;
}
statement_x;
```

Eg

```
<html>
<head>
<title> Switch Statement </title>
</head>
<body>
<script language = "javascript">
var x, n;
n = prompt("Enter value between 0 to 3");
switch(n)
{
    case '0':
            alert("zero");
            break;
    case '1':
            alert("one");
            break;
```

```
        case '2':
                alert("two");
                break;
        case '3':
                alert("three");
                break;
    default:
                alert("wrong choice");
    }
</script>
</body>
</html>
```

2. *Looping Statement*

In looping a sequence of statements are executed until some conditions for the termination of the loop are satisfied. A program loop consists of two segments. One is known as the body of the loop other known as the control statements. There are three constructs to performing loop operations.

They are:

1) The while statement
2) The do statement
3) The for statement

a) *The While Statement*

Syntax

```
while(test condition)
{
        body of the loop;
}
```

The test condition is evaluated and if the condition is true, then the body of the loop is executed. After the execution of the body, the test condition is once again evaluated and if it is true, the body is executed once again. The process of repeated execution of the body continues until the condition becomes false and the control is transferred out of the loop.

Eg

```
<html>
<head>
<title> While Statement </title>
</head>
<body>
<script language = "javascript">
var i = 1;
while(i < 20)
{
        document.write("*");
        i++;
}
</script>
</body>
</html>
```

b) The do – While Statement

Syntax

```
do
{
    body of the loop;
    }
            while(test condition);
```

On reaching the do statement, the program proceeds to evaluate the body of the loop first at the end of the loop. The test condition in while statement is evaluated. If the test condition is true, the program continues to evaluate the body of the loop once again, this process continues as long as the condition is true. If the condition becomes false the loop will be terminated and the control goes to the statement that appears immediately after the while statement.

Eg

```
<html>
<head>
<title> do – while statement </title>
```

```
</head>
<body>
<script language = "javascript">
var i = 1;
do
{
    document.write("i");
    i++;
}
while(i < = 20);
</script>
</body>
</html>
```

c) The For Statement

Syntax

```
for(initialization; test condition; increment or decrement)
    {
            body of the loop;
    }
```

The execution for the loop for loop is as follows:

1) Initialization of the control variable is done first using the assignment statement such as i = 1, constant = 1. The variables and constant are called loop controlled variables.

2) The value of the control variable is tested using the testing condition. The test condition is relational expression. The condition is true, the body of the loop is executed otherwise the loop is terminated and the execution continues with the statement that immediately follows the loop.

3) When the body of the loop is executed the control is transferred back to the for statement after evaluating the last statement in the loop control variable is incremented using an assignment statement such as i++. The new value of the control variable is again tested to see whether satisfies the loop condition.

4) If the condition is satisfied, the body of the loop is again executed this process continues till the value of the control variables fails to satisfy the test condition.

Eg

```
<html>
<head>
<title> for loop </title>
</head>
<body>
<pre>
<script language = "javascript">
var fact, i; fact = 1;
for(i = 1; i < = 5; i++)
{
     fact = fact * I;
     document.writeln(fact);
}
</script>
</pre>
</body>
</html>
```

Break and Continue Statement

Break: an early exit from the loop can be accomplished by using the break statement. When a break statement is encountered inside the loop, the loop is immediately exited and the program continues with the statement immediately following the loop.

Continue: continue is used to execute the next iteration it is optional. It does not terminate the entire loop. It terminates the block of statement in loop and continues with the next iteration.

Eg

```
<html>
<head>
<title> Break </title>
</head>
<body>
<script language = "javascript">
for(i = 0; I < 10; i++)
```

```
{
    if(i == 5)
    {
            document.write("Terminating the loop");
            document.write("<BR>");
            Break;
    }
}
document.write("Loop Terminated");
</script> </body>
</html>
```

Output

Terminating the loop

Loop Terminated

Eg

```
<html>
<head>
<title> Continue</title>
</head>
<body>
<script language = "javascript">
for(i = 0; i <= 10; i++)
{
    if(i == 5)
    {
            continue;
    }
    document.write("The value of i is" + i);
    document.write("<BR>");
}
</script>
</body>
</html>
```

The value of i is 0

The value of i is 1

The value of i is 2

The value of i is 3

The value of i is 4

The value of i is 6

The value of i is 7

The value of i is 8

The value of i is 9

The value of i is 10

UNIT–IV

JAVA SCRIPT FUNCTIONS

Functions

It is a series of commands that either calculates the value or perform an action. It consists of

1) Function name- for identification
2) Parameters- for passing the value to the function. It is optional
3) Set of commands-for performing the action when the try is called. Function can also return a value by using return keyword.

Syntax

function functionname(parameters)

{

    Javascript commands;

}

Function starts with the keyword function. All the commands that belong to a function must be placed inside the curly braces { }. Command block is referred to as function definition.

Eg

```
<html>
<head>
<title> Function </title>
</head>
<body>
<script language = "javascript">
function  display()
{
    document.write("Welcome to Java Script");
}
display();→ Calling the function
</script>
</body>
</html>
```

Passing Parameters to Functions

Here we see how to pass a parameter to a function. Parameters are listed inside the paranthesis. Each parameter is separated by a comma (,). We must send the parameters in a correct order if the function experts.

Eg

```
<html>
<head>
<title> Parameter </title>
</head>
<body>
<script language = "javascript">
var x, y, z;
function calculate(x, y)
{
    z = x + y;
    document.write("Total is" + z);
}
calculate (20 , 40);
</script>
</body>
</html>
```

Returning a Value

To return a value from the function use the return command along with the variable or value at the end of the function block.

Syntax

```
function functionname()
{
statements;
return variable or value;
}
```

Eg

```
<html>
```

```
<head>
<title> Returning a value </title>
</head>
<body>
<script language = "javascript">
var I = 6;
function x1( var x)
{
if(x % 2 == 0)
return x;
}
document.write(x1(i));
</script>
</body>
</html>
```

Scope Values

Each identifier in a program has a scope. Identifier or a variable declared inside a function have a global scope. Identifier declared outside a function has a global scope. If a local or a global variable share the name. Then the function refers variable name as local variable and not a global variable.

Eg

```
<html>
<head>
<title> Scope Value </title>
</head>
<body>
<script language = "javascript">
function ff()
{
    var  x = 10;        → local variable
    document.write(x);
}
ff();
```

```
var x = 5; → Global variable
document.write(x);
</script>
</body>
</html>
```

Templates

Syntax

```
function functionname()
{
        ...............
}
functionname();
```

Eg

```
<html>
<head>
<title> Templates </title>
</head>
<body>
<script language = "javascript">
function sum()
{
    var a = 5, b = 10;
    c = a + b;
    document.writeln( c );
}
sum();
</script>
</body>
</html>
```

Eg

```
<html>
<head>
<title> Passing Parameters </title>
```

```
</head>
<body>
<script language = "javascript">
function sum()
{
    c = a + b;
    document.writeln( c );
}
sum(5, 10);
</script>
</body>
</html>
```

Eg

```
<html>
<head>
<title> Return a value </title>
</head>
<body>
<script language = "javascript">
function sum(var a, var b)
{
    c = a + b;
    return c;
}
document.writeln(sum(5, 10) );
</script>
</body>
</html>
```

Scope Rules

1) Local
2) Global

Recursion

Call itself.

Eg

```
<html>
<head>
<title> Recursion </title>
</head>
<body>
<script language = "javascript">
function fact(n)
{
       if(n <= 1)
                 return 1;
       else
                 return(n * (n – 1)!);
}
fact(5);
</script>
</body>
</html>
```

Global Functions

1)	Escape	-	Encoding the string value. It converts the original text into hexadecimal format
2)	Unescape	-	It converts the hexadecimal format into original text
3)	Parseint	-	Convert any type into integer
4)	Parsefloat	-	Convert any type into float
5)	Eval	-	It converts alphanumeric into numeric type
6)	Isfinite	-	Checking whether the given variable is numeric or non-numeric
7)	isNAN	-	Checking whether the given variable is non-numeric or numeric

Eg

```
<html>
<head>
<title> Escape and Unescape </title>
```

```
</head>
<body>
<script language = "javascript">
var h = "script";
var x = escape(h);
document.writeln(x);
h = unescape(x);
document.writeln(h);
</script>
</body>
</html>
```

Eg

```
<html>
<head>
<title> Isfinite </title>
</head>
<body>
<script language = "javascript">
{
var n =  prompt("Enter n");
if(isfinite(n))
 document.writeln("Number);
else
document.writeln("Not Number");
}
</script>
</body>
</html>
```

Iteration vs Recursion

Iteration	Recursion
It terminates when condition fails	Base recognize
It is hard to debug	It is easy to debug
It is slower than recursion	It is faster than iteration

Arrays

Syntax

datatype variablename = new array[]

Eg

int a = new array[5]

int a = new array(5)

a[0] = 10

a[1] = 20

a[2] = 30

a[3] = 40

a[4] = 50

 (or)

int a = [10, 20, 30, 40, 50]

 (or)

int a = new Array(10, 20, 30, 40, 50)

Eg

```
<html>
<head>
<title> Array </title>
</head>
<body>
<script language = "javascript">
int a = new array(5)
for(int i = 0; i < 5; i++)
{
     a[i] = prompt("Enter a Number");
}
document.write("The values are");
for(int j = 0; j < 5; j++)

{
     document.write(a[i]);
}
```

```
</script>
</body>
</html>
```

Linear Search

1) Get the elements (n) or initialize elements.
2) Get the searching element.
3) Compare the searching elements with n elements.
4) Display the position.

Eg

```
<html>
<head>
<title> Linear Search </title>
</head>
<body>
<script language = "javascript">
int a = new Array (10)
for(i = 0; i<10; i++)
a[i] = prompt("Enter n");
int s = prompt("Enter a searching element");
for(i = 0; i<10; i++)
{
     c = 0
if(a[i] == s)
document.write("Item found in" + i + "th position");
break;
     else
               c = 1;
}
if(c == 1)
     document.write("Not found");

</script>
</body>
</html>
```

Passing Arrays to Functions

```
<html>
<head>
<title> Passing arrays </title>
</head>
<body>
<script language = "javascript">
int a = new Array(5)
a[0] = 100;
a[1] = 200;
a[2] = 300;
a[3] = 400;
a[4] = 500;
parr(a);
function parr(a)
{
    for(int i = 0; i<a.length; i++)
    document.write(a[i])
}
</script>
</body>
</html>
```

Array Functions

1) Length()   -   a length
2) Sort()   -   a sort
3) Reverse()   -   a reverse
4) Join()   -   a join

Multidimensional Array

1) Fixed array
2) Variable array

Eg

```
<html>
<head>
<title> Fixed Array </title>
</head>
<body>
<script language = "javascript">
int a = new array(2) (2)
int a = new array(2) ()
a[0] = new array(3)
a[1] = new array(3)
for(i = 0; i<2; i++)
{
     for(j=0; j<a[i].length; j++)
     a[i] [j] = prompt("Enter n");
}
</script>
</body>
</html>
```

Eg

```
<html>
<head>
<title> Fixed Array </title>
</head>
<body>
<script language = "javascript">
int a = new array(2) (2)
int a = new array(2) ()
a[0] = new array(3)
a[1] = new array(3)
for(i = 0; i<2; i++)
{
     for(j=0; j<2; j++)
     a[i] [j] = prompt("Enter n");
```

```
}
</script>
</body>
</html>
```

Javascript Objects

Object represents collections.

Object Types

1) Mathematical Object
2) String Object
3) Date and Time Object
4) Numeric and Boolean Object

Structure of Object

Syntax

objectname.methodname(parameters)

object is used for simplicity and ease of use.

Mathematical Object

Math is the object name .

1. Abs(x) → math.abs(-9) => 9

document.write(math.abs(-9))

2. Ceil(x)

It returns an integer value which is not less than x.

ceil (9.4) => 10, ceil(9.7) => 10

3. Floor(x)

It returns an integer value which is not greater than x.

Floor(9.4) => 9, floor(9.7) => 9

4. Sin(x), cos(x), tan(x)

Math.sin(45)   °

5. Pow(x, y) → x^y

Pow(2, 3) → $2^3 = 8$

6. Log(x)

Log(2) = 1.414

7. Exp(x) => e^x

8. Sqrt(x)

Math.sqrt(4) = 2

9. Round(x)

Round(6.9) = 7, round(6.3) = 6

10. Max(x, y)

Max(2, 3) = 3

11. Min(x, y)

Min(2, 3) = 2

String Object

1. charAt(index)

var s = "welcome"

s.charAt(0) = w

2. charCodeAt(index)

It returns ASCII value

s.charAt(1) = 69

3. concat(string values)

var s1 = "Web Designing"

var s2 = "Lab"

var s3 = "Program"

s1.concat(s2), s1.concat(s2,s3)

4. from charcode(values)

s1.fromcharcode(1, 5)

It returns Unicode values from the position 1 to 5 of the string value s1.

5.   Indexof(substring)

S1.indexof('e) → 2

6.   lastIndexof(substring)

s1.lastindexof('e') → 5. Because it gives preference from the last values.

7.   Indexof(substring, index)

S1.indexof('e', 3). It returns the position of e after the 3rd position.

8.   Slice(start, end)

9.   Split(string)

10. Substr(start, length)   Used to extract the substring from original string

11. Substring(start, end)

S1.slice(0, 2)

S1.split("web")

S1.substr(0, 3) →web

S1.substring(2, 5) → b

12. toLowercase()

13. toUppercase()

14. toString()

15. valueof()

s1.valueof()

Date and Time Objects

Syntax

var d = new Date()

Methods

1) getdate()
2) getUTCDate() and setDate(val)
3) getDay() and getUTCDay()

4) getFullYear() and getUTCFullYear()

5) getHours() and getUTCHours()

6) getMilliseconds() and getUTCMilliseconds()

7) getMinutes() and getUTCMinutes()

8) getMonth() and getUTCMonth()

9) getSeconds() and getUTCSeconds()

10) getTime() and getTimezoneoffset()

11) setUTCDate(val) and setFullYear(y, m, d)

12) setUTCFullYear(y, m, d) and setHours(h, m, s, ms)

13) setUTCHours(h, m, s, ms) and setMilliseconds(ms)

14) setUTCMilliseconds(ms) and setMinutes(m, s, ms)

15) setUTCMinutes(m, s, ms) and setMonth(m, d)

16) setUTCMonth(m, d) and setSeconds(s, ms)

17) setUTCSeconds(s, ms) and setTime(ms)

18) setTimezoneoffset(ms)

19) toLocateString()

20) toUTCstring()

21) toString()

22) Valueof()

Boolean and Number Objects

Var a = new boolean()

Tostring() – Boolean value 1 = string value = true and vice versa.

Valueof() – represents the Boolean object

Var a = new number()

tostring()

valueof()

Number MAX_VALUE

Number MIN_VALUE

Number NAN

Number NEGATIVE_INFINITY

Number POSITIVE_INFINITY

Document Objects

It manipulates the document which is currently available in the window.

1) Write() and writeln()
2) Cookie – it keeps track of the information which we used from beginning
3) Last modified – it returns date and time the document modified

Window Object

Open(url, name, option)

Prompt(text, default)

Close() – close the window

Focus() – activates the window

Blur() – opposite to focus

Document() – it activates the document object

Eg: Open a Child Window

Var childwindow;

Childwindow = window.open(, , resizeable = "yes", scrollbar = "yes", toolbar = "yes)

Childwindow.document.write(window.text1.value)

UNIT–V

CASCADING STYLE SHEET

Cascading Style Sheets

1) Adding styles to our web document

2) Separate from the structure of our document

3) Separate document content from the style of presentation

4) Section header, body text, links

5) Separate of structure from content greater manageability, easier to change style of document.

Syntax

```
<style type = "text/css">
      Tag {attribute: value; attribute: value}
</style>
```

Font Attributes

Attribute	Values
Font-family	A comma delimited sequence of font family names(serif, sans-serif, cursive)
Font-style	Normal, italic or oblique
Font-weight	Normal, bold, bolder, lighter or one of the nine numerical values(100, 200, ...900)
Font-size	A term that denotes absolute size, relative size, a number, percentage

Color and Background Attributes

Attribute	Values
Color	Set an elements text color. A color name or color code
Background-color	Specifies the colors in an elements background. A color name or color code.
Background-image	Set the background image. A URL or none
Background-repeat	With a background image specified setup how the image repeats throughout the page, repeat-x(repeat horizontally), repeat-y(repeat vertically), repeat(both), no repeat.

Text Attributes

Attribute	Values
Text-decoration	Add decoration to an elements text. None, underline, overline through blink.
Vertical-align	Determines an elements vertical position. Baseline, sub, super, top, text-top, middle, bottom, text-bottom and also % of the elements height.
Text-transform	Applies a transformation to the text. Capitalize, uppercase, lowercase or none
Text-align	Aligns text within an element. Left, right, corner or justify
Text-indent	Indents the first line of text. A % of elements width or length

Unit Name	Abbreviation	Explanation	Relative
EM upper	EM	The height of a font	Yes
EX lower	EX	Height of the letter x in a font	Yes
Pica	Pc	1 pica in 12 points	No
Point	Pt	1/72 of an inch	No
Pixel	Px	One dot on a screen	Yes
Millimeter	Mm	Printing unit	No
Centimeter	Cm	Printing unit	No
Inch	In	Printing unit	no

Border Attributes

Attributes	Values
Border-style	Solid, double, grove, ridge, inset, outset
Border-color	A color name or color code
Border-width	Thin, medium, thick or length
Border-top width	Thin, medium, thick or length
Border-bottom width	Thin, medium, thick or length
Border-left width	Thin, medium, thick or length
Border-right width	Thin, medium, thick or length
Border-top	Specifies width, color and style
Border-bottom	Specifies width, color and style
Border-left	Specifies width, color and style
Border-right	Specifies width, color and style
Border	Set all the properties at once

Margin Related Attributes

Attribute	Values
Margin-top	Percent, length or auto
Margin-bottom	Percent, length or auto
Margin-left	Percent, length or auto
Margin-right	Percent, length or auto
Margin	Percent, length or auto

List Attributes

Attribute	Values
List-style	Disc, circle, square, decimal, lower-roman, upper-roman, lower-alpha, upper-alpha, none

Advantages of CSS

1) Saves time.

2) Easy to change.

3) Keep consistency.

4) Use styles with JavaScript.

5) Make it easy to create a common format for all the web pages.

Style Sheets in Header Section

1) Begins with <style type = "text/css">. Style placed here for whole document.
2) Each rule body begins and ends with a curly braces {}.
3) Class declarations are preceded with a period and applied to elements only of that specific class.
4) Each property is followed by a colon and the value of property.
5) Multiple properties are separated by semicolon.

Style Sheets

1) Inline – adding styles to individual element.
2) External – adding styles to entire document and that files are stored in .css extension.
3) Embedded – adding styles within HTML document.

Inline Styles

Add styles to each tag within the HTML file. Contents and styles are missed within HTML. Use it when you need to format just a single selection in a webpage.

Eg: Inline

```
<html>
<body style = "color:yellow">
<h1 style ="font-family: arial; font-size: 40pt">
```

Cascading Style Sheets

```
</h1>
</body>
</html>
```

External Styles

Style is applied to the entire HTML file. Use it when you need to modify all instances of particular element in a web page. These style sheets are files which contain codes for providing styles to the document. This file is separately stored with .css extension. This css file can be referred by any html pages using <link> tag.

```
<link rel = "stylesheet" type = "text/css" href = "style.css">
```

Rel- relationship between original coding and style sheets.

Type – what type we used here.

Href – source code.

Eg: External

```
<html>
<body style = "color:yellow">
<h1> Cascading style sheets </h1>
<p> Cascading style sheets are used to adding styles to webpages </p>
<p class = "style">
There are 3 types of in style sheets. They are inline, external and embedded.
</p>
</body>
</html>
```

Embedded Style Sheet

Embed an entire css document in HTML head section

Eg: Embedded

```
<html>
<head>
<style  type = "text/css">
h1{font-family: Monotype Corosiva}
ul{font –style: Bold}
li{font – style: Italic}
style{background – color: blue; border – style : groove}
</style>
</head>
</body>
        <h1> Operating System </h1>
        <ul>
                <li> Introduction </li>
                <li> Types </li>
                <li> Deadlocks </li>
        </ul>
        <p class = "style">
Introduction:
```

1) Manages all hardware and software.
2) Provides controlling mechanism.

```
</p>
<p class = "style">
    Types
<ol> <li> Batch <li>
    <li> Interactive </li>
    <li> Real – time </li>
    <li> Hybrid </li>
    <li> Embedded </li>
</ol>
</p>
<p class = "style">
    Traffic Jam
</p>
</body>
</html>
```

Conflicting Styles

If we give multiple styles to the same element, conflictions will occur.

1) Users styles.
2) Authors styles.
3) Browsers styles.

To avoid the conflictions we have to give precedence to the corresponding styles.

Higher precedence – authors styles.

Parent and child relation we give higher precedence to child styles.

Positioning Elements

1) Relative – we can't move but we can declare the direction.
2) Absolute – we can move and overlap the elements.
3) Z – index is the property to overlap the elements.

Eg: Absolute

```
<html>
<head>
<style type = "text/css">
    First {position: absolute; center: 20pt; z-index: 1}
```

Second {position: absolute; center: 20pt; z-index: 2}

```
</style>
</head>
<body>
<img src = "first.gif" class = "first">
<img src = "second.gif" class = "second">
</body>
</html>
```

Eg: Relative

```
<html>
<head>
<style type = "text/css">
     super{position: relative; top: -1 ex}
     sub{position: relative; bottom: -1 em}
     left{position: relative; left: -1 ex}
</style>
</head>
<body>
Superscripted value is
X <h1 class = "super"> 2 </h1>
Subscripted value is
X <h2 class = "sub"> 2 </h2>
Left value is
X <h3 class = "left"> 2 </h3>
     </body>
     </html>
```

Background

Background-position – specifies the location top, left, bottom, right, center.

Background-attachment – contains 2 values fixed, scroll.

<span> - separates the content from parent element.

<div> - dividing the window.

Element Dimension

We can specify the dimension of the elements and document.

```
<html>
<body>
<div style = "width: 50%; height: 50%"> HTML </div>
<div style = "width: 80%; height: 20%"> JavaScript </div>
</body>
</html>
```

Box Model and Text Flow

Each block level element is called boxed elements. There are three types.

1) Padding
2) Margin
3) Border

Text flow allows elements to move from one side of the screen to other.

Media Types

Css media types allow a programmer to decide what kind of media being used to display the page. The most common media type for a web page is the screen media type which is a standard computer system. Other media types in css 2 include handheld, Braille, aural and print. The handheld medium is designed for mobile internet devices, while Braille is for machines that can read or print web pages in Braille. Aural styles allow the programmer to give a speech synthesizing web browser more information about the content of the web page. This allows the browser to present a web page in a sensible manner to a visually impaired person. The print media type affects a web pages appearance when it is printed.

Media types allow a programmer to decide how a page should be presented on any one of these media without affecting the others. A block of styles that applies to all media types, declared by @media all and enclosed in curly braces ({and})

1) Screen: standard screen technology.
2) Print: preview appearance.
3) Handheld: mobile internet services.
4) Braille: speech recognition purpose visually impaired.
5) Aural: reading and writing purpose.

It describes how the page should appear. It is used by @ media representation.

Eg

        @media screen

        @media print

        @media handheld

        @media Braille

        @media aural

        @media all

Eg

```
<html>
<head>
<style type = "text/css">
@media all
{
        Body{background-color: blue}
        P{font-size: 12pt; color: white}
}
@media print
{
        Body{background-color: white}
        P{font-size: 14pt; color: blue}
}
</style>
</head>
<body>
<p>
```

This example uses css media types to vary how the page appears in print and how its appears on any other media.

```
</p>
</body>
</html>
```

In this program we define some styles for all media types and print media types.

Building a CSS Dropdown Menu

It provides the list of linked items. Drop down menus are a good way to provide navigation links on a website without using a lot of screen space. The important property is display property. This allows a programmer to decide whether an element is rendered on the page or not. Possible values include block, inline and none. The block and inline display the element as a block element or an inline element while none stops the element from being rendered.

Display Property

1) Blocked – boxed elements
2) Inline – specific to the particular part
3) None

Eg

```
<html>
<head>
<style type = "text/css">
Body{font-family: arial, sans-serif}
Div menu{font-weight: bold; color: white}
Div menu: hover a{display: block}
Div menu a{display: none; border-top:2 px solid #225599; background-color: white}
Div menu a: hover{background-color: #dfeeff}
</style>
</head>
<body>
<div class = "menu"> Menu
    <a href = "#"> Home </a>
    <a href = "#"> News </a>
    <a href = "#"> Articles </a>
    <a href = "#"> Blog </a>
    <a href = "#"> Contact </a>
</div>
</body>
</html>
```

In this program a div of class menu has the text "Menu" and 5 links inside it. This is our drop down menu.

The behavior we want is a s follows:

1) The text that say "Menu" should be the only thing visible on the page, unless the mouse is over the menu div.

2) When the mouse enters or hovers over the menu div, we want the links to appear below the menu for the user to choose form.